The Secret History of Emotion

The Secret History
of Emotion

From Aristotle's « Rhetoric » to Modern Brain Science

DANIEL M. GROSS

The University of Chicago Press ❋ *Chicago and London*

DANIEL M. GROSS
is assistant professor
of rhetoric at the
University of Iowa. He is
coeditor of *Heidegger and
Rhetoric.*

The University of Chicago Press, Chicago 60637
The University of Chicago Press, Ltd., London
© 2006 by The University of Chicago
All rights reserved. Published 2006
Printed in the United States of America
15 14 13 12 11 10 09 08 07 06   1 2 3 4 5
ISBN: 0-226-30979-7 (cloth)

An earlier version of chapter 1 was previously
published as "Early Modern Emotion and the
Economy of Scarcity," *Philosophy and Rhetoric* 34,
no. 4 (2001), 308–21. Copyright 2001 by The
Pennsylvania State University, reproduced by
permission of the publisher.

Library of Congress Cataloging-in-Publication Data

Gross, Daniel M., 1965–
    The secret history of emotion : from Aristotle's
rhetoric to modern brain science / Daniel M. Gross.
        p.   cm.
    Includes bibliographical references and index.
    ISBN 0-226-30979-7 (cloth : alk. paper)
    1. Emotions—Social aspects—History.
2. Emotions (Philosophy)—History.   I. Title.

    BF531.G76 2006
    152.409—dc22   2005026553

To my son Max Gross—
living proof that emotions are never one's own

Contents

Acknowledgments

The seed of this project germinated in the mid-1990s while I was finishing my graduate work in the rhetoric department at the University of California, Berkeley. During this period, Judith Butler, Félipe Gutterriez, Victoria Kahn, Hans Sluga, Nancy Struever, John Tinkler, and Hayden White nurtured a project that would emerge only upon my departure. A dissertation year at Tübingen University in Germany on a DAAD Fellowship, where I was sponsored by Gert Ueding of the Seminar für Allgemeine Rhetorik, advanced my work on the phenomenology of emotion and gave me access to early modern material unavailable elsewhere.

The project crystallized during my two years as Andrew W. Mellon Postdoctoral Fellow at the University of California, Los Angeles, where I enjoyed formal association with the UCLA Humanities Consortium (Center for Seventeenth- and Eighteenth-Century Studies), the Department of English and the Department Comparative Literature at UCLA, the William Andrews Clark Memorial Library, and the Getty Research Institute for the History of Art and the Humanities, which in 1998 shared "passions" with the UCLA Humanities Consortium as a topic of special inquiry. From this period I thank for their input and support Tom Albrecht, Page duBois, Martha Feldman,

Philip Fisher, Lawrence Green, Stefan Jonsson, Reinhart Meyer-Kalkus, Vincent Pecora, Peter Reill, Kenneth Reinhard, Michael Roth, Debora Shuger, Elaine Scarry, Jonathan Sheehan, Bill Viola, and Michael Witmore.

The University of Iowa has provided a thrilling environment in which to finish the project. My polemic against cognitive scientists of emotion is impassioned because I completed the book at Iowa, where first-rate cognitive scientists of emotion do their work. Likewise, my methodological commitment runs deep because I completed the book at Iowa, where rhetorical inquiry is especially rich and takes many forms. For providing the time and the environment to complete my project, I thank the Project on Rhetoric of Inquiry (POROI), Jay Semel and an Obermann Center for Advanced Studies Research Seminar Stipend, a Bloomington Eighteenth-Century Workshop Grant, and the support of the rhetoric department and the College of Liberal Arts and Sciences. For their feedback on the project in its various incarnations, I thank Barbara Biesecker, Aimee Carrillo Rowe, David Depew, Eric Gidal, Joshua Gooch, Philip Gross, John Nelson, John Peters, Takis Poulakos, Laura Rigal, Adam Roth, Alvin Snider, Bridget Harris Tsemo, Vershawn Ashanti Young, Russell Valentino, and McClain Watson.

Finally, I thank Douglas Mitchell at the University of Chicago Press for his distinct editorial vision, and my wife, Carla Wilson, for her thoughtful conversation.

Introduction:
A New Rhetoric of Passions

If you are tickled to learn that Aztecs located passions in the liver, here is something at least as quaint from René Descartes: "The ultimate and most proximate cause of the passions of the soul is none other than the agitation with which the spirits move the little gland which is in the middle of the brain"— that is to say, the pineal gland. Or so Descartes proposes in his 1649 treatise on the passions composed for Princess Elizabeth of Bohemia. Now compare this to Aristotle's *Rhetoric*, where, for instance, anger is defined as "desire, accompanied by . . . distress, for conspicuous retaliation because of a conspicuous slight that was directed, without justification, against oneself or those near to one" (1378a31–33).[1] For Aristotle, anger (*orge*) may indeed be

---

1. Aristotle, *On Rhetoric: A Theory of Civic Discourse*, trans. and ed. George A. Kennedy (New York: Oxford University Press, 1991). For a discussion of the translation of this passage, see the excellent collection of essays *Ancient Anger: Perspectives from Homer to Galen*, ed. Susanna Braund and Glenn W. Most (Cambridge: Cambridge University Press, 2003), esp. 17, 100, 123; see also W. W. Fortenbaugh, *Aristotle on Emotion* (London: Duckworth, 2002). James R. Averill's *Anger and Aggression: An Essay on Emotion* (New York: Springer, 1982) cites Aristotle centrally in building a social constructivist model of emotion in psychology (340).

accompanied by physical distress—say the boiling blood expressed in crimson cheeks—but its proximate cause is anything but that little gland in the middle of the head. Anger is a deeply social passion provoked by perceived, unjustified slights, and it presupposes a public stage where social status is always insecure. Concretely what does this mean? And what secret history of emotion will this contrast unfold? It means that anger is constituted not in the biology nor even in the dignity all humans are supposed to share equally, but rather in relationships of inequity: "Great is the rage of Zeus-nurtured Kings," muses Aristotle after the *Iliad* 2.196. For Aristotle, the king does not fly into a rage simply because his human dignity suffers, or even because his power allows him to express a universal emotion others suppress. The king is overcome by rage because he suffers a concrete insult despite belonging to the class of people who "think they are entitled to be treated with respect by those inferior in birth, in power, in virtue," which in the king's case means practically everybody (1378b35).

Like other emotions, ranging from the most obviously social (such as love and jealousy) to those that are supposed to be hardwired (such as fear and disgust),[2] Aristotle's anger requires a series of enabling conditions obscured by our platitudes of biology and universal human rights. (1) Anger presumes a *public stage* rather than private feelings. Alone on a desert island, the king would not be subject to anger, because he would lack any social standing that might be concretely challenged; indeed, he would not be a king at all. Likewise, an inconspicuous slight in a public forum—say, the king imagined with no clothes—cannot provoke

---

2. Paul Ekman, *Emotions Revealed: Recognizing Faces and Feelings to Improve Communication and Emotional Life* (New York: Holt, 2003), 11–12. I will move back and forth in this study between the terms *passion* and *emotion* without invoking a strict distinction. However, the more familiar term *emotion* will generally signal a contemporary perspective, while the antiquated term *passion* will indicate either a historical perspective or vehemence, which is how the term is typically still used today. For a thorough discussion, see Thomas Dixon, *From Passions to Emotions: The Creation of a Secular Psychological Category* (Cambridge: Cambridge University Press, 2003).

the king's desire for conspicuous retaliation. (2) Anger assumes *asymmetrical power.* Some are perfectly entitled to belittle others and can expect no anger in return, while others, such as the slave, are entitled to none of the pride that would make them susceptible to anger. In other words, anger, according to Aristotle, is directed at those who have no right to belittle, and "inferiors have no right to belittle" (1379b12). (3) Aristotle's anger does not presume our familiar psychological individual whose feelings are expressed in a fit. And despite its cognitive moment ("he thinks . . . "), the king's anger is not the expression of an opinion, as Stoics and some contemporary philosophers would argue.[3] Rather, its presumptions are thoroughly psycho*social.* The king is angry because his entitlement is concretely threatened, and without that extracognitive entitlement manifest in the world around him, the king would have no angry thoughts at all. And that brings me to a final point linking Aristotle directly to early modern psychologists such as Thomas Hobbes, David Hume, and William Perfect, or even to someone like Judith Butler in our day. (4) Aristotle's anger presumes *a contoured world of emotional investments,* where some people have significantly more liabilities than others. A man becomes angry both at those who belittle him and, interestingly, at those belittling others whom it would be shameful for him not to defend, such as parents, children, wives, or dependents (1379b29). Emotional investments running the other direction are meager at best.

3. For instance, Richard Sorabji, *Emotion and Peace of Mind: From Stoic Agitation to Christian Temptation* (Oxford: Oxford University Press, 2000). My perspective does overlap with Robert C. Solomon's influential work on emotion as constitutive of experience, but it diverges from his cognitive perspective that collapses at crucial points into a decisionism that forecloses adequate historical and political analysis of emotion. Addressing the right topic in the wrong way, Solomon writes, "It is important to stress once again that . . . personal status, like all the structures of our emotional mythologies, is *constituted* in our judgments. However much we may seek and search for friends and equals, ultimately we decide to *make* them such." *The Passions: Emotions and the Meaning of Life* (Indianapolis: Hackett, 1993), 208. What this perspective obscures are the social institutions of "judgment" built into the legal system, for instance, which dramatically constrain individual decisions about equality and inequality.

Reading Aristotle, or for that matter most canonized literature up to the nineteenth-century social realism of Émile Zola
and Charles Dickens, might give one the impression that people from a lowly station have no emotions at all, let alone the
emotions of social responsibility, such as magnanimity or angry
indignation.[4] As Aristotle famously observes in the *Poetics*, the
finest tragedies—which is to say, the tragedies that most dramatically exorcise emotions of pity and fear—are "always on the
story of some few houses," such as Oedipus, because the misfortune of someone better than us matters most (1453a–1454a15).
Likewise, we might consider why the tragedy of Princess Diana's
death could provoke mourning across the world while the death
of an indigent provokes apathy or, more accurately, nothing at
all. The contours of our emotional world have been shaped by
institutions such as slavery and poverty that simply afford some
people greater emotional range than others, as they are shaped
by publicity that has nothing to do with the inherent value of
each human life and everything to do with technologies of social
recognition and blindness. One goal of this study is to explain
how these technologies of emotion work.

I would not want to defy common sense along the way by
insisting that an actual child or a wife or a dependent such as a
slave cannot become angry. Medea would suggest otherwise, and
even in Aristotle's scheme each social subordinate would have
the capacity for anger directly in proportion to the scope of his
or her justifiable pride. Moreover, in chapter 4, where I read
Sarah Fielding's sentimental novel *David Simple* as a response
to David Hume's *A Treatise of Human Nature*, I show that the
very terms of emotion such as pride and humility are contestable.
Brilliant though they are, Aristotle's and Hume's elitist theories

4. In his classic study *The Passions and the Interests: Political Arguments for
Capitalism before Its Triumph* (Princeton, NJ: Princeton University Press, 1997), Albert
O. Hirschman remarks in passing that early modern statecraft was particularly concerned with bridling the passions of the powerful because the powerful were believed
to be "particularly well endowed with passions in comparison to the lesser orders" and
could therefore do harm on a huge scale (69–70).

of emotion are not "right" in some metaphysical sense. They do, however, provide a lucid critique of power that reminds us that the democratization of emotion over the last two centuries is incomplete at best and a model of distraction at worst. Following Aristotle and Hume, it is useful to think about how the scope of anger afforded a social subordinate is strictly limited to the vanishing point in a world where pride is also limited (as it is, for instance, in Hume's and Fielding's Britain, where pride is considered a function of property and strictly limited by custom and law to a narrow segment of the population). Throwing a temper tantrum or fuming or muttering curses under one's breath might strike us as a lesser degree of the same emotion exercised by a vengeful tyrant who forces a defiant subject to eat his own son for dinner,[5] but it would not strike Aristotle so. And we would do well to pay close attention to Aristotle and his early modern relatives if we hope to see our way beyond the current platitudes of emotion.

So where did we get the idea that emotion is a kind of excess, something housed in our nature aching for expression? In part from *The Passions of the Soul* (1649), where Descartes proposed the reductive psychophysiology of emotion that informs both romantic expressivism and latter-day sciences of the mind and brain. Indeed, one goal of this book is simply to recall that we do not just naturally express emotions converging on our amygdala or wherever, but rather that we are first constituted as expressive agents by what the philosophers of the Scottish Enlightenment called "social passions." Contrary, however, to these optimistic philosophers such as Francis Hutcheson and Adam Smith, who tried to anchor social passions in a moral sense equally shared by all, I argue that the constitutive power of emotions depends upon their uneven distribution. By looking at the rhetoric of this un-even distribution in any particular case—for instance, in the case of Aristotle's apathetic slave, Seneca's angry tyrant, Hobbes's re-sentful preacher, Sarah Fielding's humble hero, or Adam Smith's

---

5. An example from Seneca's *On Anger*, revisited in chapter 2.

compassionate spectator—we rediscover a critical tool obscured by the science of emotion and underdeveloped in the study of literature.[6]

My project is distinguished by its rhetorical approach, which puts the question of politics front and center. In chapter 1, I work primarily with Aristotle's *Rhetoric* and Thomas Hobbes to outline a "political economy" wherein passions are (1) constituted as differences in power,[7] and (2) conditioned not by their excess, but by their scarcity. Though we may reject the conclusions reached by Aristotle or Hobbes, their rhetorical analysis of emotion allows us to address important questions neutralized in the Cartesian paradigm. In chapter 2, I push this analysis of emotion one step further in the direction of the humanities by considering apathy as a productive political category rather than as a personal moral failing. Far from signaling a general retreat from politics, Stoic apathy in the work of Seneca and Hobbes's antagonist Henry More turns out to be a prerequisite for the distribution of political passions to some and not to others. Complementing the first two chapters on the dubious triumph of emotional Cartesianism, chapter 3 also advances my genealogical project of reconstituting social emotions by first showing how they have been obscured: in this case, by a late-modern fixation on masculine political agency asserted at the expense of political "passivism," now relegated to

6. Notable exceptions include Alan T. McKenzie, *Certain Lively Episodes: The Articulation of Passion in Eighteenth-Century Prose* (Athens: University of Georgia Press, 1990); and Adela Pinch, *Strange Fits of Passion: Epistemologies of Emotion, Hume to Austen* (Stanford, CA: Stanford University Press, 1996).

7. This Foucauldian element of my work on the social construction of emotion I share with certain anthropologists, notably Lila Abu-Lughod, *Veiled Sentiments: Honor and Poetry in a Bedouin Society* (Berkeley: University of California Press, 1986); and especially Catherine A. Lutz, whose *Unnatural Emotions: Everyday Sentiments on a Micronesian Atoll and Their Challenge to Western Theory* (Chicago: University of Chicago Press, 1988) complements my history of emotion in the West. Whereas Lutz contrasts the Western view of emotion as "in essence a psychobiological structure and an aspect of the individual" with the local Ifaluk theory and practice of emotion as "*index of* social relationship" (4), I find the theory and practice of emotion as an index of social relationship *in* the West, though now hidden behind the view of emotion as a psychobiological structure and an aspect of the individual.

a diminished femininity (*passive*, also from the Latin root *passio*). In this chapter I read sermons to the rebellious Long Parliament (1640–1660) in order to show how a nonreductive, early modern understanding of social passions was incapacitated by a radicalized late-modern active/passive dyad, which we now tend to read back inappropriately into the early modern context. Taken together then, the first three chapters illuminate the negative space or "shadow economy" of emotion characterized by apathy, passivity, and humility.

In chapters 4 and 5, I focus on the dyad of pride and humility, and finally compassion, as I extend my historical analysis of emotion into the eighteenth-century literature of sensibility, especially the work of David Hume, Sarah Fielding, Adam Smith, and William Perfect. I then ask how this historical analysis informs our most suggestive psychoanalytic theories of emotion. For it turns out that Hume can help us do what Judith Butler urges in *The Psychic Life of Power*: to think a theory of power together with a theory of the psyche. Like Hume's humble woman whose very sense of self is already constituted by the narratives and institutions that subordinate her, Butler's melancholic has already withdrawn into the psyche "a configuration of the social world" that subordinates the subject from the inside, so to speak. Both Hume and Butler challenge the notion of autonomous will and psychological universalism, asking instead what losses are compelled by culturally prevalent prohibitions (notably for Hume patriarchy and for Butler heteronormativity) and what culturally prevalent forms of psyche result. But despite being structured in similar ways, the humble and the melancholic are not the same sort of people after all, which means that their political diagnosis and therapy will differ as well. In fact, reading Hume against Butler encourages us to identify the precise history of the humble soul's object relations and figure out how the humble psyche is therefore *different* from that of the melancholic, the apathetic, and so on.

At the broadest level, my historical thesis is that overtly political rhetoric in the context of the English Civil War was transformed into an implicit epistemology in the Age of Sensibility and beyond. Seventeenth-century political rhetoric, in other words, became a generalized psychology thereafter, and passions that were once overtly rhetorical, such as anger, pride, and humility, now quietly gird the Western system of belief that emotion is hardwired to the human nature we all share equally. Or even more prosaically, one might imagine emotions that were once treated by everybody as externalized forms of currency and worldly investments sucked, as it were, into the brain. The goal of the book is, therefore, twofold: first, to reconstitute by way of critical intellectual history a deeply nuanced, rhetorical understanding of emotion that prevailed until the triumph of psychophysiology; second, to show by way of literary and philosophical example how this rhetorical perspective helps us read anew the emotional complex of modernity, whether early or late. In doing so, I demonstrate that early modern theories of emotion in the Aristotelian vein can inform Judith Butler's recent efforts to integrate politics and psychoanalysis.

My hope is that this book can contribute to a new rhetoric of passions analogous to the new rhetoric of tropes introduced by Paul de Man and other deconstructionists in the 1970s.[8] In recent years, literary critics working primarily in the European and American Age of Sensibility have revisited emotion both to argue for its social construction and, even more recently, to argue contrarily for its biology.[9] In literary studies, intellectual

---

8. Most important are Jacques Derrida, "White Mythology: Metaphor in the Text of Philosophy," in *Margins of Philosophy*, trans. Alan Bass (Chicago: University of Chicago Press, 1982), 207–71, first published in *Poétique* 5 (1971); and Paul de Man, *Allegories of Reading: Figural Language in Rousseau, Nietzsche, Rilke, and Proust* (New Haven, CT: Yale University Press, 1979).

9. Here I should introduce Eve Kosofsky Sedgwick's and Adam Frank's formidable attack on social construction launched in "Shame in the Cybernetic Fold: Reading Silvan Tomkins," which first appeared in *Critical Inquiry* (1995) and then was republished in Sedgwick's *Touching Feeling: Affect, Pedagogy, Performativity* (Durham, NC: Duke University Press, 2003). Fed up with the likes of Ann Cvetkovich and other foot soldiers of Foucault and Greenblatt, Freud and Lacan, Lévi-Strauss, Derrida, and the feminists, who seem to equate "theory" with the simple claim "*It's not natural*" (109), Sedgwick

history, philosophy, anthropology, and psychology, emotion has emerged as a topic of central importance, apparently because it promises access to the domain of protoreason previously obscured by methodologies such as rational choice in the human sciences or linguistic analysis in the humanities. No doubt, references to Aristotle's *Rhetoric* are common across the literature on emotion, while in literary studies per se one is not surprised to see the sentimentalism of *Uncle Tom's Cabin* excused in terms of peculiarly nineteenth-century rhetorical theories of community feeling.[10] Rarely, however, do scholars in either the human sciences or the humanities appeal adequately to the rhetorical tradition for insight into the emotions, despite the fact that rhetoric was the first, and remains the richest, resource for such inquiry.

Surprisingly, the same can be said for the field of rhetorical studies as it is typically practiced in U.S. English and communication studies departments. Some study of emotion is certainly expected in these fields, where the first priority is to teach college freshmen the skills of persuasive speaking and writing: just like textbooks from the Roman *ad Herennium* to those of the nineteenth-century British elocutionary movement,

and Frank return in this essay to the work of maverick psychologist Silvan Tomkins, who accounts for differences in affect in terms of the "density of neural firings" (102). Or, more charitably, Sedgwick and Frank endorse Tomkins because, unlike Theory with a capital *T*, which cannot differentiate among affects, Tomkins can account for qualitative differences among different affects by emphasizing "the inefficiency of the fit between the affect system and the cognitive system—and between either of these and the drive system—that enables learning, development, continuity, differentiation" (107). I believe Sedgwick and Frank make their mistake when they claim that theory cannot differentiate among affects or posit any nonarbitrary relation between representation and the thing represented (for instance, *pride* and pride) without rediscovering cybernetics or something like Tomkins's biology. Theory can meaningfully differentiate between different affects (or passions, or emotions), and even between different instances of the same affect, by way of *history*: a possibility Sedgwick and Frank overlook in their essay despite ambivalent appreciation for a master of history and theory, Michel Foucault. See Ann Cvetkovich, *Mixed Feelings: Feminism, Mass Culture, and Victorian Sensationalism* (New Brunswick, NJ: Rutgers University Press, 1992).

10. Jane P. Tompkins, "Sentimental Power: *Uncle Tom's Cabin* and the Politics of Literary History," in *Uncle Tom's Cabin* (New York: Norton, 1994), 511.

contemporary rhetoric textbooks immediately advise students to master appeals to emotion, such as opening a speech or essay with a moving anecdote. Even the recent theoretical turn to "constitutive rhetoric" typically fails to integrate the rhetoric of emotion with the effort to develop a more sophisticated model of persuasion that situates rhetoric in culture rather than in the intentions of the orator or author.[11] I hope that my new rhetoric of passions will be useful to the field of rhetorical studies insofar as it demonstrates how historical work can be important, indeed necessary, for strong rhetorical criticism.

How, then, do I use the term *rhetoric* in this study? Most importantly, I want to convey how rhetoric is at once an embedded cultural practice and an inventive attitude which allows us to reflect critically upon those very same cultural practices. Like other classical terms *philosophy* and *medicine*, *rhetoric* can refer to a concrete practice ("mere rhetoric"), a practitioner (the rhetorician), a discursive quality ("the rhetoric of passions"), and a theory (the content of Aristotle's *Rhetoric*). Like classical poetics, the inventive attitude distinguishes rhetoric from philosophy, which has the basic attitude of description, and from medicine, which shares with rhetoric the basic attitude of intervention. Indeed, a dramatic new possibility for rhetorical invention opened when the ancient discipline was adopted in European early modernity. And since this important story for my work has never been told adequately, I will take a moment to do so.

For Aristotle, rhetoric's function is not to teach a particular code of behavior, nor even to persuade; instead, it is defined as "an ability [*dynamis*], in each case, to see [*theoresai*] the available means of persuasion" (1355b27–28). Rhetoric for Aristotle is a theoretical art of human nature extracted from everyday legal and political practice. Elsewhere I argue in more detail that

---

11. The classic essay is Maurice Charland's "Constitutive Rhetoric: The Case of the *Peuple Quebecois*," *Quarterly Journal of Speech* 73 (1987): 133–50. See also James Boyd White, *Heracles' Bow: Essays on the Rhetoric and Poetics of the Law* (Madison: University of Wisconsin Press, 1985).

the modern turn opens Aristotle's understanding of rhetoric to history, realizing possibilities dormant in classical antiquity and forgotten again in the nineteenth century, when rhetoric was largely reduced to the study of figures and tropes or the art of personal persuasion.[12] For convenience, we might say that after Nicolas Caussin's brilliant history of rhetoric, *Eloquentia sacrae et humaneae parellela* (1619), "the available means of persuasion" were no longer confined theoretically to a psychological domain of shared beliefs, hopes, and fears. Now persuasive power could be related explicitly to historical and cultural context, and what we now call "speech situations" could be understood in historical terms.

Caussin's method is philological. In a fascinating chapter, *De nomine Rhetorum*, Caussin asks what the "rhetor" did in a range of cultural settings and what *rhetoric* signified. Homer's discussion of Phoenician oratory is treated briefly, and legal rhetoric is traced to its origins in the composition of the so-called Doric laws. Then, with the introduction of classical rhetoric, Caussin's historical narrative begins in earnest. To be a rhetorician in the Athenian Golden Age was to "lead the people" in all important matters of state: *Rhetores duces populi*. Rhetoric played a crucial role in policy deliberation, war, political council both foreign and domestic, in taxation, writing laws, and in the law's administration. Thus, the name "rhetorician" was honorable, suffering no indignities when compared to the poet or philosopher—and this despite Plato's notorious confusion of rhetoricians and sophists in the *Gorgias*. However, according to Caussin, it was precisely the power of rhetoric in a republican system that led to its professionalization, and thus eventually to its downfall. Ambitious students understood the power of eloquence and were willing to pay a premium for good training in public oratory. Ambitious but short-sighted teachers of rhetoric set up independent

---

12. Daniel M. Gross, "Metaphor and Definition in Vico's *New Science*," *Rhetorica* 14, no. 4 (1996): 359–81; "Caussin's Passion and the New History of Rhetoric," *Rhetorica* 21, no. 2 (2003): 89–112.

schools and became ever more preoccupied with promoting their own system by walling it off from competitors. Though Caussin praises the rare skill and honor of a few rhetoric teachers such as Isocrates and Demetrius, he sees the age increasingly dominated by the precious and affected rhetoric of the schools (*orationis delicias*). On the other hand, rhetoric under the Roman emperors was generally "lascivious," despite the need for effective administration of the provinces. Imperial rule obstructed public debate, and ingenious minds were forced to find expression in mere linguistic games and meaningless bickering. "Thus when liberty was crushed, those who were formerly principal figures in the state, rhetoricians of great repute—judges in matters most noble—degenerated into litigious squabblers in petty cases."[13] In the Roman Empire a tremendous gap had opened between eloquence human and divine, and into this gap stepped Paul.

The methodological consequences of Caussin's historical semantics are profound. Rather than simply weighing the achievements and failures of ancient rhetoric against a contemporary standard, as did the late Humanists such as Joachim Camerarius or Nicodemus Frischlin, Caussin ties emotional discourse to particular cultural milieus. Rather than forcing a veil of inevitability upon his narrative, Caussin takes an interest in explaining, for instance, how a contingent fact such as the greed and hubris of certain sophists precipitated a general decline in Greek eloquence. From this philological method, a breathtaking set of possibilities emerges. Though God may be the ultimate source of sacred eloquence, human eloquence is bound to a historical situation. This meant that political rhetoric would have to be sensitive to more than the immediate situation in which it functioned and reflexive not just as a rule-bound practical art. It would now have to be reflexive with respect to its own historical situation and

---

13. "Extincta igitur libertate, illi, qui prius erant civitatis principes magni nomnis Rhetores, aut causarum illustrium disceptatores, in caussularum litigiosos actores degenerarunt." Nicolas Caussinus, *Eloquentia sacrae et humaneae parellela* (Paris: Chappelet, 1619), 6.

characterize how things might be otherwise. This is a "rhetoric of the possible" in a distinctly modern vein.

From Giambattista Vico we then learn how historical rhetorics provide unique access to the history of emotion. In his *New Science* (1725; cited 3rd ed., 1744), Vico takes the "moving force" of rhetoric, spelled out traditionally in terms of passionate orators, and draws out the consequences of *movere* for collective, historical being. In one important case, he describes how a particular sort of being is first identified in terms of metaphor (an illegitimate child is a "monster") and then defined in an institutional framework that seals this historical subject's fate (Roman law in the age of the Twelve Tables demanded that a "monster" of this sort be thrown into the Tiber river). So in Vico's scheme an illegitimate child would not become an official threat just because some were convinced of its monstrosity. Fear of this sort might still have disastrous consequences for a child, but those consequences would not be categorical; other illegitimate children would not necessarily have to die. However, when passion became institution, when fear was written into law as a way to protect patrilineal inheritance, illegitimate children were moved in their very identity. What we have then is persuasion of a sort tangential to individuals and intentions, or even to an audience collected in a public forum. But it is nonetheless persuasion of the strongest sort. We can call it institutional persuasion.

Vico's example presents the double movement of rhetoric that defines its modern possibility. Vico applies rhetorical *analysis* to a historical moment in which a particular kind of rhetorical *activity* becomes institution—in this case a moment in which social passion is articulated in law. One advantage of a rhetorical approach is that interpretation thus remains appropriately scaled. The danger (or promise, depending on one's perspective) is that rhetoric encourages a skeptical attitude toward the very institutions it helps compose. Historical rhetorics remind us that, however real and consequential they might be, the institutions that help shape us are ultimately of our own making and therefore are subject to change. In his example, Vico describes not the power of rational persuasion in the courtroom or assembly, but a more diffuse power that comes in the staging of a social drama where there are consequences to the descriptions under which people fall, the roles they play, and the differences through which they are marked. Among other things, we can take away from Vico's example the understanding that rhetoric defines a field of social actors rather than merely giving predefined subjects something clever to say in public.

"Political rhetoric" would then run deeper than a politician's hollow pitch, and we would look for political dynamism beyond the representative public sphere. An important facet of historical research requires rhetorical analysis that can map the relationship between the formal and the political. A political culture is defined in part by rhetorical possibilities: its figurative self-portrait, its political ontology, its laws of inclusion and exclusion, its commonplaces and clichés. Simply contrasting rhetoric with reality echoes the cleverly misleading claims of some Baroque rhetoricians that eloquence is just a decorous addition to reality defined within the parameters of courtly life: the rhetoric of love taught to average citizens so that they can better sing the praises of the Prince, the rhetoric of sympathy so that fellow underlings might be consoled. Then as now, the role that rhetoric plays in routinizing communication and delineating channels of social power can be obfuscated by an appeal to aesthetic niceties. Obscured thereby is the constitutive function of rhetoric that may seem ornamental, such as Christian Weise's massive *Politischer Redner*,[14] which devotes three hundred pages to the art of the compliment, or the rhetorical handbooks that specify what salutation is appropriate for a letter to a nobleman's wife, a political nemesis, or a Jew. Rhetoric is mistakenly viewed as the mere expression of real politics—never its substance—while critical strategies for parsing the political body are religiously ignored. Vico's example can

14. Christian Weise, *Politischer Redner / Das ist: Kurtze und eigentliche Nachricht Wie ein sorgfältiger Hofmeister seine Untergebene in der Wohlredenheit anführen soll...* (Kronberg: Scriptor, 1974).

help us see instead how a stratum of social reality is accessible only by understanding the particular rhetorics at play. And when we understand how the rhetoric of a particular social reality is put together, it becomes all the more clear how things might be different.

As opposed to univocal speech that would mean the same thing everywhere, rhetoric is always in brackets, whether that means it is a public statement subject to skepticism, a truth claim subject to counterevidence or counterargument, a law subject to contextual interpretation or historical revision, or even a poetic expression or image that "makes a world" and is therefore subject to remaking. Despite being embedded in relatively stable institutions, from the law to visual stereotypes, rhetoric always represents the possibility that things might be otherwise. Incidentally, that is also why rhetoric always carries with it the potential for theory and education, both of which are practices that exploit the gap between any particular rhetorical formulation and its possibilities (for example, possibilities of meaning, of context, of reception, of revision).

Finally, as opposed to the philosophy that posits language as a mirror of nature, rhetoric is an inventive attitude toward language and the world, where "emotion" names one important way in which language and the world connect. Without the anxiety of patriarchy, there would be no Vichian "monster." Without privileged access to the emotions of pride, anger, and magnanimity, there would be no Aristotelian "king." For rhetoricians, emotion makes language and identity matter. I have already shown that Aristotle understood emotional investments as thoroughly rhetorical rather than simply a reflection of one's god-given, or even one's preordained, social status. Emotions are the contours of a dynamic social field manifest in what's imagined and forgotten, what's praised and blamed, what's sanctioned and silenced. After all, that is why the most detailed treatment of the emotions appears in Aristotle's *Rhetoric* rather than in his treatises on *The Parts of Animals* or *The Movement of Animals* or elsewhere in his logic and natural science, though fascinating discussions of emotion appear in the latter as well. Materialized in brains, faces, bodies, and even in objects and architecture, such as a tombstone or an amusement park, emotions clearly exceed the merely ideal. But neither are emotions essentially material. Instead, the most appropriate way to approach emotions is phenomenologically, as Martin Heidegger suggests in his fascinating commentary on Aristotle's *Rhetoric*,[15] which means starting with the concrete manifestation of emotion in a *meaningful* world, as opposed to a world of mere matter. In this meaningful world, rhetoric will then be the leading art, as opposed to the more abstract arts of logic and mathematics or the material practices of hard science.

And because emotion for Aristotle is a rhetorical construct first, one is obligated as a skilled analyst to consider its fragile aura and its failures as well as its clear expression. Those who have the special luxury of taking pride in their appearance, for instance, are susceptible to a special sort of anger that is heightened "if they suspect they do not really have [what they take pride in], either not at all or not strongly, or do not seem to have it" (1379a35). In other words, the anger of ugliness comes not from some physical truth, but rather from the anxiety that surrounds self-perception. Anger is a rhetorical construct manifest in the anxious iteration of one's appearance broadly understood to include reputation, and it is subject always to the deflating threat of gossip or insult, whether real or imagined. Moreover, as a rhetorical construct, emotion can be bound to surprising reversals of fortune that dramatically exceed the individual and function at the level of cultural institutions and their histories. Consider in our time the beleaguered "angry white male" who has rediscovered his violent passion as an antidote to feminism and

15. In his 1927 masterwork *Being and Time*, Martin Heidegger writes, "this work of Aristotle (the *Rhetoric*) must be taken as the first systematic hermeneutic of the everydayness of Being with one another." *Being and Time*, trans. John Macquarrie and Edward Robinson (New York: Harper & Row, 1962), 178. For commentary on this now famous passage and its background in Heidegger's 1924 lecture course on Aristotle's *Rhetoric*, see Daniel M. Gross and Ansgar Kemmann, eds., *Heidegger and Rhetoric* (Albany: SUNY Press, 2005).

black power, but this time with a pathetic twist missing when the white man was supposedly king. Indeed, under the right conditions, emotion can be appropriated precisely by those who would have it denied: think for instance of the political work exercised today in "gay pride," where the emotion David Hume once tied to social value became a rallying point for those who would have no social value at all.

A few warnings and a final exhortation. To begin with, we must take care when asking how generally the psychosocial, Aristotelian view of emotion was held in the eighteenth century or elsewhere. At least since the Enlightenment, explicit claims about human nature's consistency across time and place do regularly serve as rhetorical gestures that directly contradict the analysis of emotion that typically follows, where instead what matters are distinctions of class, culture, social status, and so forth. No doubt the Aristotelian, psychosocial view of emotion is not held widely at all by the time you reach the eighteenth century, and in our day it is held by very few—indeed, it is practically impossible to articulate coherently insofar as it has disappeared behind the post-Enlightenment liberal and scientific views. Practically speaking, however, psychosocial emotions remain in the textual fabric along with some of the habits of mind and turns of phrase that emerged in its heyday of explicit recognition (which I locate in mid-seventeenth-century political rhetoric), often causing distortions in the liberal and scientific texts that appear later, including some of the most notoriously universal, such as Alexander Pope's *An Essay on Man* or Adam Smith's *Theory of Moral Sentiments* or in Samuel Johnson's *Rambler*. Right after Johnson praises the pleasures and vexations of Shakespeare's passions "communicable to all times and to all places" or regrets the miseries common across the human species, for instance, he can follow with a nuanced sociopolitical analysis of vanity that dramatically qualifies, if it does not outright contradict, the principle of universal emotion. When Johnson observes in the *Rambler* 66 (1750) that vanities of wealth, power, and reputation "must be always, by their own nature, confined to a very small number," he admits that the greater part of humankind will lead very different emotional lives. It turns out that human nature, in this case and in others I will treat, serves primarily as a rhetorical placeholder, not as a consistent analytic principle. And it is this tension in the text that is then subject to my rhetorical criticism or, for that matter, to the criticism of any who might try their hand. The point, finally, is not to make someone like Samuel Johnson into a consistent social constructivist of emotion nor to ignore his principled generalizations, but rather to suggest by way of significant example how all sorts of supposedly universal texts are rejuvenated when read with the social sensibilities of Aristotle in mind.

Although the theoretical component of this study will sometimes demand that I consider Aristotle's *pride* and Hume's *pride* and gay *pride* the same thing, it should be remembered that each use of the term implicates a particular history. If we assume that each use of the term *pride* refers unequivocally to the same thing, not only have we lost our ability to critique theories of universal human emotion, but we have also lost our ability to say anything at all about the culture of pride that interested me in the first place. For instance, understanding gay pride, including its moment of emergence after Stonewall in the 1970s, its reference to a newly formed political subculture, its capacity to frighten and motivate, has everything to do with the particular history whereby pride was wrested from the grip of those who would customarily have a monopoly. The same must be said of other key terms in this study: *apathy, passivity,* and *humility.* Only by treating them historically will we be able to figure out at what cost to our political sensibilities these terms of emotion (and its absence) were transformed from civic virtues into civic vices.

Another note on terminology and history. Unlike Joseph LeDoux, who develops an important argument that "emotion" is not a coherent category because fear differs from an emotion like jealousy in terms of its physiology, its place in evolutionary biology, and in its purpose, and unlike literary and cultural historians who argue that "emotion" is no longer a useful category because it obscures particular histories of shame, guilt, melancholy, and so on, I will continue to use this generic term *emotion* and its relative *passion* primarily in contrast to *reason*. Though I will strategically draw sharp distinctions between my key emotional terms and even between different references to "the same" emotion, my discussion of the "reason versus passion" topos in chapter 2 will show how giving up the category of emotion completely would make some important theoretical work and even some historical work impossible.

While Aristotle and surprisingly like-minded psychologists of early modernity such as Hobbes and Hume will help demonstrate how emotions are strategic, all (except for Fielding) stop short of theorizing how emotion can turn against the powerful. However, their unblinking critique of power makes this last step easy—much easier in fact than liberal theories of universal human dignity or scientific theories of emotion such as Antonio Damasio's, which incidentally does try to explain how antisocial emotions such as ethnic hatred should eventually disappear like our tailbone. After all, how might the brain science of emotion help us understand a cultural phenomenon such as gay pride or the angry white male or ethnic hatred without reducing it beyond recognition? Despite the vigorous effort of someone like Damasio, it can't, and that is why I spend some time in the following pages showing how Damasio's evasion of rhetoric writes itself into his science, where it begs for our deconstruction. I take this same deconstructive approach in my critique of Martha Nussbaum's *Upheavals of Thought: The Intelligence of Emotions* (2001), which represents our most sophisticated liberal humanist theory of emotion. It is important to realize, however, that deconstruction cannot gain traction in these cases without specifying the history that sanctions and shapes the evasion of rhetoric in contemporary brain science and beyond: namely, the turn from seventeenth-century political rhetoric to eighteenth-century psychology. Only an awareness of this history allows one to see exactly what the cost is to our intelligence when, like Adam Smith in *The Theory of Moral Sentiments*, we *begin* to think about emotion in terms of what we all share equally as human beings.

Hence this final exhortation as well. By telling the story of our psychophysiology of emotion and by showing at what cost it emerged, I hope to provide access once again to the rich rhetoric that still quietly shapes our emotional world for worse and for better.

1

Early Modern Emotion and the Economy of Scarcity

Descartes's Brain

We can learn a good deal about the rhetoric of human nature in early modern Europe simply by asking what passions were. When we do, we find not only that their descriptions disagree but also that the things described as passions seem incommensurable. Are passions tangible "things" residing in the soul, or are they dispositions of the heart, or beliefs of the mind? Is passion a matter of personal expression, or is it something essentially social that a person performs? Do they come from our interior, or from the things we perceive? Can they be measured and manipulated— their causes controlled—or do passions elude control by their very nature? Are they divine, diabolical, or human, and can we distinguish them according to their origin? Are they the enabling condition of virtue or its enemy? Are they necessary or disposable? What is their number and what do they do? Exasperated by endless wrangling over such questions, Descartes complains

There is nothing in which the defective nature of the sciences which we have received from the ancients appears more clearly than in what they have written on the passions; for although this is a matter which has at all times been the object of much investigation, and though it would not appear to be one of the most difficult, inasmuch as since every one has experience of the passions within himself, there is no necessity to borrow one's observations from elsewhere in order to discover their nature. (331)[1]

With this preliminary remark, Descartes renders human nature in its quintessential modern form: it is something housed in a body and subject to the self-evidence of a descriptive science. According to Descartes, what we know is best established through introspection, and so is what we feel. Everyone has experience of the passions "within himself," and therefore it is unnecessary to borrow one's observations from elsewhere in order to discover passion's nature. But ultimately for Descartes introspection is not about attaching meaning to our emotions in the narrative form of autobiography. It is not like Hobbes's dictum *"Nosce teipsum, Read thy self,"* a prelude to the radical mutation of human nature required for commonwealth (*Leviathan*, 10),[2] nor is it a primitive form of psychoanalytic introspection. Rather, it is a literal "look-inside" the body. Thus, to control those passions that have unfortunately been trained to vice, we must better understand body mechanics.

To do so, according to Descartes, it is helpful first to identify human activity independent of those passions that are the

---

1. René Descartes, *The Passions of the Soul*, in *The Philosophical Works of Descartes*, trans. E. Haldane and G. R. T. Ross (Dover: Dover Publications, 1955); for commentary on Descartes and the passions, see also Nancy S. Struever, "Rhetoric and Medicine in Descartes's *Passions de l'âme*: The Issue of Intervention," in *Renaissance-Rhetorik / Renaissance Rhetoric*, ed. Heinrich F. Plett (Berlin: de Gruyter, 1993); Susan James, *Passion and Action: The Emotions in Seventeenth-Century Philosophy* (Oxford: Clarendon, 1997); Jeffrey Barnouw, "Passions as 'Confused' Perception or Thought in Descartes, Malebranche, and Hutcheson," *Journal of the History of Ideas* 53, no. 3 (1992): 397–424; David Summers, "*Cogito* Embodied: Force and Counterforce in René Descartes's *Les passions de l'âme*," in *Representing the Passions: Histories, Bodies, Visions*, ed. Richard Meyer (Los Angeles: Getty Research Institute, 2003).

2. Thomas Hobbes, *Leviathan*, ed. Richard Tuck (Cambridge: Cambridge University Press, 1991).

soul's motivating force. Certain sorts of movements—such as the blinking of an eye threatened by a poking finger—cannot be affected even by our knowledge that the finger belongs to a benign friend. In this case, the machine of our mind is useless because "the machine of our body is so formed that the movement of this hand towards our eyes excites another movement in our brain, which conducts the animal spirits into the muscles which cause the eyelids to close" (338). Articles 2 through 16 of Descartes's *The Passions of the Soul* further explain body mechanics independent of the soul, including its heat and movement; its vitality and death; the role of blood circulation, muscles, nerves, the heart, and animal spirits; as well as the "little tubes," or *vincula*, that transport animal spirits between body and brain.

If body mechanics work on reflex, passions are for Descartes forms of retardation. Unlike actions originating from within—thirst and hunger, for example—passions of the soul provide space for learning, memory, and judgment. If, for instance, we see some animal approach us, and

if this figure is very strange and frightful—that is, if it has a close relationship with the things which have been formerly hurtful to the body, that excites the passion of apprehension in the soul and then that of courage, or else that of fear and consternation according to the particular temperament of the body or the strength of the soul.... For in certain persons that disposes the brain in such a way that the spirits reflected from the image thus formed on the gland, proceed thence to take their places partly in the nerves which serve to turn the back and dispose the legs for flight, and partly in those which so increase or diminish the orifices of the heart. (348)

Passions are thus defined as the "perceptions, feelings, or emotions of the soul which we relate specially to it, and which are caused, maintained, and fortified by some movement of the spirits" (344). And since passions are produced by the movement of blood and spirits, they are also accompanied by legible signs, the most salient of which are actions of the eyes and face, changes of color, tremors, languor, swooning, laughter, tears, groans, and sighs (381).[3]

But, we might ask with Spinoza, is there not a domain of freedom inserted into the causal chains of human activity?[4] How does Descartes explain why people respond to the same situation differently—some with consternation and some with courage— in the face of a similar physical threat? Ostensibly Descartes does make room in the mind for both divine ideas and debased habits of thought. But social difference ultimately has no causal efficacy in the explanation of behavioral variation. Physical differences alone explain why the same causes can excite different passions in different people: "The same impression which a terrifying object makes on the gland, and which causes fear in certain men, may excite in others courage and confidence; the reason of this is that all brains are not constituted in the same way" (349). Even when it comes to a passion that seems intuitively social, such as love, Descartes brackets out the intentional world of things loved and people loved, focusing his analysis instead on the consistent physiology of love. "There is also no need to distinguish as many kinds of love as there are diverse objects which we may love; for, to take an example, although the passions which an ambitious man has for glory, a miser for money, a drunkard for wine, a brutal man for a woman whom he desires to violate, a man of honour

3. For the legacy of Cartesian expressivism in the physiognomy of classical French painting, see Charles Le Brun, *A Method to Learn to Design the Passions* (Los Angeles: William Andrews Clark Memorial Library, 1980). See also Charles Darwin, *The Expression of the Emotions in Man and Animals*, introduction, afterword, and commentaries by Paul Ekman, 3rd ed. (1872; Oxford: Oxford University Press, 1998). Darwin's work, designed to bolster his evolutionary theory by showing a continuity of emotional expression across species, has recently regained credibility due to Ekman's endorsement. Ekman claims Darwin as an ally in his battle against cultural relativists in the tradition of Margaret Mead. For a strong critique of Ekman's project, see John McClain Watson, "From Interpretation to Identification: A History of Facial Images in the Sciences of Emotion," *History of the Human Sciences* 17, no. 1 (2004): 29–51.

4. Baruch Spinoza, *Ethics*, in *Spinoza: Selections*, ed. John Wild (New York: Scribner's, 1958), 366. On the relation of Spinoza's theory of the passions to that of Descartes, see Genevieve Lloyd, *Part of Nature: Self-Knowledge in Spinoza's Ethics* (Ithaca, NY: Cornell University Press, 1994), 77–104.

for his friend or mistress, and a good father for his children, may
be very different, still, inasmuch as they participate in love, they
are similar" (367).

But strict mechanical determinism is untenable in a world that
includes both divine principles and human failings. At a certain
point we must take responsibility for our behavior without simply
blaming a God or an evil demon. Descartes thus seems compelled
to suggest a remedy for excesses of passion that exploits human
volition and the power to judge right and wrong: "what we can
always do on such occasions, and what I think I can here put
forward as the most general remedy and that most easy to practice
against all excesses of the passions, is that, when we feel our blood
to be thus agitated, we should be warned of the fact, and recollect
that all that presents itself before the imagination tends to delude
the soul" (426). A weak remedy indeed, as the monist Spinoza
was quick to point out, and one reminiscent of the Stoic Seneca's
urging that we fight anger with moral "precepts": *Ira praeceptis
fugatur* (see chapter 2). For it is a remedy that locates the entire
transaction of otherwise independent mind and body in that small
portion of matter called the pineal gland—a remedy that requires
second-order conscience to chase after first-order feelings.

As we can surmise from Spinoza's unenthusiastic reply,
Descartes's theory of remediating the passions received a lukewarm response from his contemporaries and from later theorists of the passions as well. However, the outline of Descartes's
psychophysiology of emotion still carries substantial weight—
indeed, the picture Descartes paints still seems familiar. Despite
his misnomers and mechanical blunders, and despite his unavoid-
able ignorance of the evolutionary theory that has since taken
center stage in the science of emotion, Descartes's mechanical
model translates into late-modern terms. For the sake of comparison, here's how, in *Scientific American*, a leading neuroscientist of
emotion, Joseph LeDoux, describes a response to danger (fig. 1):[5]

5. Reprinted in Joseph LeDoux, *The Emotional Brain: The Mysterious Underpinnings
of Emotional Life* (New York: Simon & Schuster, 1996), 166.

The Misleading Scientific Model

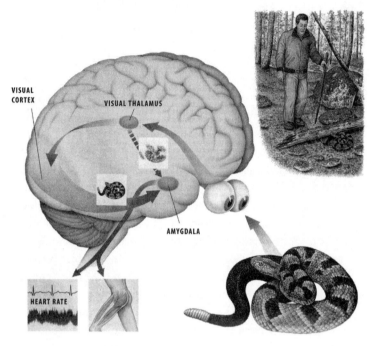

FIGURE 6-14   Brain Pathways of Defence.

As the hiker walks through the woods, he abruptly encounters a snake coiled up behind a log on the path (upper right inset). The visual stimulus is first processed in the brain by the thalamus. Part of the thalamus passes crude, almost archetypal, information directly to the amygdala. This quick and dirty transmission allows the brain to start to respond to the possible danger signified by a thin, curved object, which could be a snake, or could be stick or some other benign object. Meanwhile, the thalamus also sends visual information to the visual cortex (this part of the thalamus has a greater ability to encode the details of the stimulus than does the part that sends inputs to the amygdala). The visual cortex then goes about the business of creating a detailed and accurate representation of the stimulus. The outcome of cortial processing is then fed to the amygdala as well. Although the cortial pathway provides the amygdala with a more accurate representation than the direct pathway to the amygdala from the thalamus, it takes longer for the information to reach the amygdala by way of the cortex. In situations of danger, it is very useful to be able to respond quickly. The time saved by the amygdala in acting on the thalamic information, rather than waiting for the cortical input, may be the difference between life and death. It is better to have treated a stick as a snake than not to have responded to a possible snake. Most of what we know about these pathways has actually been learned by studies of the auditory as opposed to the visual system, but the same organizational principles seem to apply. (From J. E. LeDoux, Emotion, memory and the brain. *Scientific American* [June 1994], vol 270, p. 38. © 1994 by Scientific American Inc., all rights reserved.)

FIGURE I. The above image and caption are Joseph LeDoux's, as published in *The Emotional Brain*.

"As the hiker walks through the woods, he abruptly encounters a snake coiled up behind a log on the path" (Descartes's hapless victim likewise encounters a strange and frightful animal). Immediately, the visual stimulus is processed in the brain by the thalamus, which passes "crude, almost archetypal, information directly to the amygdala" (while Descartes's spirits reflected from the image form on the pineal gland). "This quick and dirty transmission allows the brain to start to respond to the possible danger signified by a thin, curved object, which could be a snake" (whereas Descartes refers to the perceived object's "close relationship with things that have been formerly hurtful to the body"). Meanwhile, the thalamus also sends visual information to the visual cortex, which "goes about the business of creating a detailed and accurate representation of the stimulus" (just as Descartes's "soul" imposes a more thoughtful judgment between stimulus and response). The snake as an "emotionally competent object"—to anticipate Antonio Damasio's term—thus precipitates the cascade of events that become the emotion we call fear, and finally behavioral, autonomic, and endocrine responses manifest as a bodily response to evident danger (while Descartes's nerves dispose the legs for flight).

So instead of Descartes's hydraulics of animal spirit, we can now talk in terms of endocrinology; instead of locating the passions in the pineal gland alone, we look for them in a complex of brain sites converging on the amygdala. Descartes's explanation of perception and nervous reaction seems broadly accurate, as does his gambit to relocate emotions from the heart to the mind. Even LeDoux's distinction between cerebral and noncerebral emotional reactions—which has proven so attractive to philosophers of emotion and pop psychologists alike because it lends itself to theories of "emotional intelligence"[6]—was itself anticipated by Descartes in his distinction between simple reflex and a full emotional response that depends upon thought and a

6. Daniel Goleman, *Emotional Intelligence* (New York: Bantam, 1995); Sorabji, *Emotion and Peace of Mind*, 62 (see introduction, n. 3).

lifetime of experience. We can, then, isolate in *The Passions of the Soul* at least two principles that shape the human nature we take for granted today.

First, instead of an Aristotelian soul composed of hierarchically organized and interdependent vegetable, animal, and human functions, Descartes identifies an indivisible soul with the mind. Where the soul was once a complex entity irreducible to either mind or body, now its functions could be redistributed dualistically. But when its functions are thus redistributed, the soul loses altogether its significance as an object of scientific inquiry. When we wish to identify and analyze the essential elements of human nature—that is, when we want to follow up on Descartes's famous clock metaphor and find out what "makes us tick"—we turn either to the mind, if we are philosophers, or to the brain, if we are empirical psychologists. The "soul," where the term still functions at all, is relegated to the religious domain. There the material strata assumed by Aristotelian theologians such as Philipp Melanchthon are dropped, and the soul is confined instead to that part of the human being that is immaterial, immortal, and divine. Second, as Descartes sees it, passions are something "in" us that we express; they are mental dispositions that tie perception to action. Thus, when we want to analyze the passions, we call them "emotions" and read their physiological signs. In this way a certain side of experimental human science emerges in its modern form, modeled on the natural sciences. Unfortunately, both of these principles make it more difficult for us to see the logic of emotion beyond its physical manifestation—more difficult, that is, to see in what ways emotions are *irreducibly* social.

The Limits of Brain Science

As Ian Hacking remarks in a *Times Literary Supplement* review of Joseph LeDoux's *The Emotional Brain*, "sciences that study the emotions are in fine fettle."[7] Indeed, this flurry of activity has

7. Ian Hacking, "By What Links Are the Organs Excited?" *Times Literary Supplement*, July 17, 1998, 11–12.

produced some interesting results, by any measure. LeDoux's work, for instance, has done a good job explaining how the range of phenomena we typically categorized as "emotions" in fact vary dramatically in terms of their appearance in the evolutionary saga and thus in their physiology as well. Damasio's work on the emotional life of brain-damaged patients has produced some useful therapies and has made inroads against mind/body dualism in Western medicine by showing concretely how judgment and emotion are connected. However, these successes— which have impressed even leading humanists such as Martha Nussbaum, Philip Fisher, and Richard Sorabji[8]—have perhaps emboldened brain scientists to expand their theories of emotion to a (dramatically impoverished) social world, at the expense of a more nuanced, humanistic perspective of the sort initiated by Aristotle and assumed, to great advantage, in a wide range of early modern literature. The story of amygdala-damaged "S," as told by Antonio Damasio in *The Feeling of What Happens: Body and Emotion in the Making of Consciousness*, deserves scrutiny at this point because it illustrates perfectly how brain science of emotion goes awry when it blunders into social fact.[9]

"Almost a decade ago," Damasio recounts, "a young woman, to whom I shall refer as S, caught my attention because of the appearance of her brain CT scan." Her scan revealed that, although most of her brain was perfectly normal, both amygdalae were calcified to the extent that little or no normal function of neurons within the amygdalae was possible (62). Damasio then shifts abruptly from the objective to the subjective standpoint: "My first impression of S was of a tall, slender, and extremely pleasant young woman" (63). OK. Being charitable, one might concede that first impressions matter for Damasio because he is

8. Martha Nussbaum, *Upheavals of Thought: The Intelligence of Emotions* (Cambridge: Cambridge University Press, 2001); Sorabji, *Emotion and Peace of Mind* (see introduction, n. 3); Philip Fisher, *The Vehement Passions* (Princeton, NJ: Princeton University Press, 2002).

9. Antonio Damasio, *The Feeling of What Happens: Body and Emotion in the Making of Consciousness* (New York: Harcourt, 1999).

interested in social emotions, and therefore his own immediate response to her tall, slender, pleasant looks is relevant. But there is more. After explaining that S had no problem learning new facts, Damasio recounts that her social history, on the other hand, was "exceptional": "To put it in the simplest possible terms, I would say that S approached people and situations with a predominantly positive attitude" (64). For instance, Damasio offers, shortly after an introduction, S would not shy away from hugging and touching. But "make no mistake," Damasio reassures the reader, "her behavior caused no discomfort to anyone." And as it turns out, this forthcoming (but evidently not unpleasant) behavior pervaded all areas of her life. "She made friends easily, formed romantic attachments without difficulty, and had often been taken advantage of by those she trusted." It was as if, Damasio explains, emotions such as fear and anger had been removed from her affective vocabulary (65), and therefore she had failed to learn the "significance of the unpleasant situations that all of us have lived through," failed to learn the "telltale signs that announce possible danger and possible unpleasantness, especially as they show up in the face of another person or any situation" (66). In characterological terms, we might observe, the supposedly generic man (or monkey, as LeDoux would have it) who startles at a snake now becomes a slender woman with boundary issues.

Of course, S's story is more than idiosyncratic, according to Damasio. The connection between amygdala damage and fear as an appropriate social emotion is supposedly proved in a study published in *Nature* by Damasio and his colleagues that required a "judgment of trustworthiness and approachability based on human faces." And here, in my opinion, Damasio's account becomes quite troubling. As Damasio describes it, this experiment called for the judgment of one hundred human faces that had been previously rated by "normal individuals" as indicating varied degrees of trustworthiness and approachability. The selection of these faces was made by normal individuals who were asked a supposedly simple question: "How would you rate this face on the scale of one to five, relative to the trustworthiness and approachability that the owner of the face inspires? Or, in other words, how eager would you be to approach the person with this particular face if you needed help?" As it turns out, Damasio tells us that S, along with other amygdala-damaged patients, "looked at faces that you or I would consider trustworthy and classified them, quite correctly, as you or I would, as faces that one might approach in case of need. But when they looked at faces of which you or I would be suspicious, faces of persons that we would try to avoid, they judged them as equally trustworthy" (66–67).

I have no reason to doubt that the human amygdala triggers socially relevant information in response to visual stimuli, as the authors of the study claim.[10] S's calcified amygdalae may have indeed affected her socially. It is even plausible that her fear response was affected most of all. But you don't have to be a classical humanist or a critical race theorist to find all this a bit unsettling. When the social model used to analyze a brain-damaged patient's abnormality is so impoverished, a host of new problems are thereby introduced into the experiment and beyond, into both its interpretation and its application to theories of a larger social world. Since when, to begin with, are trustworthiness and approachability unambiguous indicators legible on an unfamiliar face? Isn't trustworthiness, for instance, essentially a matter of shared experience? And which faces? Judged by whom? How does the "I" in the "you and I" change who might be considered a friendly face in times of need? How, in this case, can the scientists establish a "normal" judgment, when there is no statistically valid sample that can be reliably purged of race, gender, age, cultural bias, and so on? It is as if the racist and anti-Semitic blunders of nineteenth-century physiognomy had never

10. Ralph Adolphs, Daniel Tranel, and Antonio R. Damasio, "The Human Amygdala in Social Judgment," *Nature* 393 (1998): 470–74. Subjects were asked to imagine meeting the person on the street and to indicate how much they would want to walk up to that person and strike up a conversation. Normal controls were University of Iowa undergraduates: 16 males, 30 females; the study supposedly controls for gender but nothing else.

happened, the biases of contemporary racial profiling somehow becoming controllable in the twenty-first-century laboratory.

Given Damasio's proleptic statements on the limits of science and his repeated claim that he is not attempting to reduce so-cial phenomena to biological phenomena,[11] one is tempted to dismiss these forays into social theory as misguided addenda to otherwise sound science. But the problem runs deeper than that, to the very heart of Damasio's experimental program. First of all, it is no accident that trustworthiness gets stripped of its essentially social quality. Though Damasio likes to cite literary figures such as Shakespeare and T. S. Eliot epigraphically, when it comes to seriously analyzing a "secondary" or social emotion such as an embarrassment, jealousy, guilt, pride, or, for that matter, the feeling of trust, literary insight gives way to evolutionary biology and "secondary" emotions reduce to "primary": happiness, sad-ness, fear, anger, surprise, and disgust (51). Drawing upon the scientific psychology of Paul Ekman, author and editor of influ-ential studies from "Pan-Cultural Elements in Facial Displays of Emotion" (1969) to *What the Face Reveals* (1997),[12] Damasio can normalize a trustworthy face and ignore its social construction because, *for his limited purposes*, a human face can be treated as a more complicated version of the snake encountered above. The ability to read a human face "correctly"—that is, to judge whether the face is attached to a person who potentially means well or harm—is, according to Damasio, an adaptive human trait shared by everyone with a normal brain. Recalling Descartes's lack of interest in the love object (as opposed to the experience of love), brain scientists of emotion argue that, in experimental terms, it doesn't matter what the competent object of emotion might be, whether snake or stick, black face or white. After all, prejudice *is* built into the snap judgment, sometimes for good reason; our

---

11. Antonio Damasio, *Descartes' Error: Emotion, Reason, and the Human Brain* (New York: Quill/HarperCollins, 2000), xviii, 124.

12. P. Ekman, E. R. Sorensen, W. V. Friesen, "Pan-Cultural Elements in Facial Displays of Emotion," *Science* 164 (1969): 86–88; Paul Ekman and Erika Rosenberg, eds., *What the Face Reveals* (New York: Oxford University Press, 1997).

physiological bias against coiled snakes and snarling dogs helps us survive just as does our physiological bias against those who appear different.[13] To localize emotion in the body, what matters to Damasio is only where the subject of the experiment falls in a normal pattern: for instance, if her prejudices map normally onto the subject pool, chances are her emotional brain is in fine shape; if not, not. However, when an experiment designed to characterize normal brain function *in a social setting* strips its measurable marker (i.e., the subject's judgment of trustworthiness) of its inherent sociality, the question of normal brain function is begged. Like all social phenomena, it is precisely the variable nature of judging trustworthiness and approachability that makes them social phenomena in the first place, as opposed to, say, phenomena that are more immediately physiological, such as thirst and hunger. Though one might stipulate a technical definition that allows acontextual comparisons across categories of race, gender, and age, thereby producing verifiable measurements, common usage and common sense tell us that the judgment of trustworthiness and approachability is irreducibly about who I am, who you are, and what circumstances prevail. Control for these factors in an experiment (which is certainly doable in theory), and the phenomenon you want to study disappears.

As a humanist defending the autonomy of interpretive social studies,[14] the point I wish to make in this book is not that subjective experiences like emotion resist scientific study because of some mystical quality.[15] Instead, I suggest that subjective

13. See Damasio, *Descartes' Error*, 133, 173–74, on somatic markers; Antonio Damasio, *Looking for Spinoza: Joy, Sorrow, and the Feeling Brain* (New York: Harcourt, 2003), 40, 163, on evolutionary mechanisms for detecting social difference.
14. *Humanism* I understand in the tradition running from Giambattista Vico, *The New Science of Giambattista Vico*, trans. Thomas Goddard Bergin and Max Harold Fisch (Ithaca, NY: Cornell University Press, 1968); through Wilhelm Dilthey, *Introduction to the Human Sciences: An Attempt to Lay a Foundation for the Study of Society and History*, trans. Ramon J. Betanzos (Detroit: Wayne State University Press, 1988); and Hans-Georg Gadamer, *Truth and Method*, trans. Joel Weinsheimer and Donald G. Marshall (New York: Crossroad, 1989).
15. Damasio's critique in *Feeling of What Happens*, 309.

experiences such as emotion have an essential social component and are best treated with *social analysis* of the sort developed in the rhetorical tradition, not scientific analysis that must reduce social phenomena in certain critical ways so as to function properly as science. Despite Damasio's protest against the reduction of social to biological phenomena, he nevertheless delivers the following reductive claims on a regular basis: "Love and hate and anguish, the qualities of kindness and cruelty, the planned solution of a scientific problem or the creation of a new artifact are all based on neural events within a brain" (*Descartes's Error*, xvii); "For most ethical rules and social conventions, regardless of how elevated their goal, I believe one can envision a meaningful link to simpler goals and to drives and instincts" (*Descartes's Error*, 125); "Our identities are displayed in sensory cortices, so to speak" (*Feeling of What Happens*, 223); or even more prosaically, "We still need digestion in order to enjoy Bach" (*Feeling of What Happens*, 125). Indeed, the passage from Spinoza's *Ethics* that frames the personal narrative of Damasio's later work and provides the dramatic climax is given a similar turn. According to Damasio, Spinoza's proposition that "the very first foundation of virtue is the endeavor to preserve the individual self, and happiness consists in the human capacity to preserve its self (*virtutis fundamentum esse ip sum conatum proprium esse conservandi, et felicitatem in eo consistere, quòd homo suum esse conservare potest*) contains, implausibly, the foundation for a system of ethical behaviors rooted in neurobiology (*Looking for Spinoza*, 170).

I will concede that it is *trivially true* and therefore uninteresting to assert that everything human, including the judgment of trustworthiness, has some localizable and theoretically measurable manifestation in the body or brain.[16] Damasio and his

---

16. In fact, Damasio winds up defining emotion as Descartes does, in a combination of behaviorist and mechanistic terms: though for the sake of his most recent book, *Looking for Spinoza*, "emotions are actions or movements, many of them public, visible to others as they occur in the face, in the voice, in specific behaviors" (28), an "emotion-proper," such as happiness, sadness, embarrassment, or sympathy, is finally considered a "complex collection of chemical and neural responses forming a distinctive pattern" (53).

fellow neuroscientists of emotion are indeed studying something interesting to do with the amygdala and other brain functions tied up with the experience and expression of emotion. But they are not studying the social brain with an adequate understanding of what it means to be social, and they are certainly not improving society, as Damasio ultimately wishes to do. In fact, Damasio's main purpose in *Looking for Spinoza: Joy, Sorrow, and the Feeling Brain* is to show how "an understanding of the neurobiology of emotion and feelings is a key to the formulation of principles and policies capable of reducing human distress and enhancing [to cite Martha Nussbaum[17]] human flourishing" (8). Despite Damasio's poetic sensibility and good intentions, one shudders to imagine what such a society might look like.

Here is the question for a brain scientist working within the parameters of evolutionary theory: when a damaged brain isn't the cause, what produces poor judgments of character such as the judgment made by the vast majority of Germans in 1933 that Adolf Hitler was a trustworthy leader and Jews untrustworthy (the sort of social problem that has long concerned Damasio in his more expansive moods)? Adaptive prejudices are relatively easy to explain in terms of the platitudes of evolutionary biology such as "regulating the life process" and "promoting survival" (*Looking for Spinoza*, 35), maladaptive prejudices less so. As I have already discussed, Descartes ventured that people react differently to emotional triggers because their brains are configured differently. Considering that his first book is called *Descartes's Error*, it is fair to ask whether Damasio can do any better explaining emotional variation. You may already suspect that I think not. More important is that his failure is characteristic of scientists who attempt social theory without shifting gears.

Once again, the story becomes disturbing as the scientist moves quantitatively from amoebas to UNESCO without ever shifting the *qualitative* mode of analysis in a manner appropriate to different things—an error Damasio commits most egregiously

17. Nussbaum, *Upheavals of Thought*, 4.

in his discussion of homeostasis and the governance of social life (*Looking for Spinoza*, 166–69). "All living organisms," explains Damasio, "from the humble amoeba to the human are born with devices designed to solve *automatically*, no proper reasoning required, the basic problems of life." These problems include finding sources of energy, maintaining a chemical balance of the interior compatible with the life process, maintaining the organism's structure by repairing its wear and tear, and fending off external agents of disease and physical injury (30). That's fine. However, the regulation of adult human life, Damasio admits, "must go beyond those automated solutions because our environment is so physically and socially complex that conflict easily arises due to competition for resources necessary for survival and well-being" (166). More easily than for other organisms? I would ask. Now "simple processes such as obtaining food and finding a mate become complicated activities" (again the question is begged, what has changed qualitatively?) and these are joined by many other "elaborate processes" such as manufacturing, commerce, banking, health care, education, and insurance. Moreover, Damasio asserts, our life must be regulated not only by our desires and feelings but also "by our *concern* for the desires and feelings of others expressed as social conventions and rules of ethical behavior." But take careful note. Instead of drawing upon a social theory appropriate to these more complex human institutions, Damasio simply reduces something like a social or political contract to an extension of the "personal biological mandate" (173). Social conventions and the institutions that enforce them—religion, justice, and sociopolitical organizations—become for Damasio simple mechanisms for exerting homeostasis at the level of the social group. In fact, as Damasio sees it, social institutions from the World Health Organization to UNESCO and the United Nations are all essentially institutions that "promote homeostasis on a large scale (169)."

What, then, about "sick cultures," as Damasio calls them, such as Germany and the Soviet Union during the 1930s and 1940s, China during the Cultural Revolution, Cambodia during the Pol

Pot régime (*Descartes's Error*, 178), or even our own sick culture rife with sexism, racism, and other, shall we say, maladaptive biases? How does one determine scientifically what a sick culture is, after all? And returning now to Damasio's more limited project, what barriers to objectivity are faced by the brain scientist of emotion who works within a sick culture? This is called the paradox of the observer: how can one adequately characterize an abnormal emotional brain when one's study might be designed within a sick culture or at least in a culture affected by maladaptive biases inherently unidentifiable and therefore uncontrollable from within the scientific study? Surprisingly, Damasio concedes in *Descartes's Error* that (*a*) "the buildup of adaptive somatic markers requires that both brain and culture be normal" (177), while (*b*) sizable sectors of Western society are gradually becoming tragic counterexamples to the norm (179). Nine years later, in *Looking for Spinoza*, Damasio obscures this fatal flaw in his experimental program, but without much success. Now Damasio combines some sociobiology with the superficial optimism of the Scottish Enlightenment and a dash of Stoic moralism. As Seneca and Descartes advised before him, Damasio suggests that we can simply learn how "some emotions are terrible advisors and consider how we can either suppress them or reduce the consequences of their advice."

> I am thinking, for example, that reactions that lead to racial and cultural prejudices are based in part on the automatic deployment of social emotions evolutionarily meant to detect *difference* in others because difference may signal risk or danger, and promote withdrawal or aggression. That sort of reaction probably achieved useful goals in a tribal society but is no longer useful, let alone appropriate, to ours. We can be wise to the fact that our brain still carries the machinery to react in the way it did in a very different context ages ago. And we can learn to disregard such reactions and persuade others to do the same. (40)

Even as a rhetorician, I don't have nearly the same faith as Damasio in the power of persuasion.

"Each and every occasion of negative emotion and subsequent negative feeling places the organism in a state outside its regular range of operations," Damasio explains (139). And something like justified fear is an "excellent insurance policy" that has saved or bettered many lives. "But," Damasio continues inexplicably, "the engagement of anger or sadness is less helpful, personally and socially." Well-targeted anger can discourage abuse and act as a defensive weapon "as it still does in the wild." In many social and political situations, however, anger is "a good example of an emotion whose homeostatic value is in decline." In fact, Damasio concludes on a wildly optimistic, Smithian note, "the history of our civilization is, to some extent, the history of a persuasive effort to extend the best of 'moral sentiments' to wider and wider circles of humanity, beyond the restrictions of the inner groups, eventually encompassing the whole of humanity" (163).

Unobjectionable claims often mask a more insidious reality. Though he projects that neurobiology will play an important role in future explanations of social phenomena, Damasio, in a conciliatory mood, does admit that a simple neurobiological explanation for the rise of ethics, religion, law, and justice is "hardly viable" (159). In order to comprehend these cultural phenomena satisfactorily, Damasio recognizes that we need ideas from anthropology, sociology, psychoanalysis, and evolutionary psychology, as well as findings from studies in the fields of ethics, law, and religion. "In fact," Damasio ventures, "the course most likely to yield interesting explanations is a new breed of investigations aimed at testing hypotheses based on integrated knowledge from any and all of these disciplines *and* neurobiology." Glance, however, at the footnote to learn what project Damasio champions as this new breed of investigation that brings together biology and the humanities, and there one finds in fact the *pièce de résistance* of E. O. Wilson's virulent sociobiology, *Consilience*.[18]

---

18. Edward O. Wilson, *Consilience: The Unity of Knowledge* (New York: Knopf, 1998).

Damasio's error and the limits of brain science of emotion should now be clear as they pertain both to the scientific project narrowly conceived and to the larger social project. Next I will introduce more fully the humanistic alternative as it developed in the rhetorical tradition and shaped, among other things, early modern political theory.

Rhetoric as the Aristotelian Alternative

Overlooked in our late-modern romance with natural science is the influence of Aristotle's ethical and rhetorical theory of the passions on seventeenth-century political thought and beyond. Though the Englishman Thomas Hobbes is perhaps the most well known of the bunch, a theory of the passions that can be construed as broadly Aristotelian reaches from the late sixteenth-century Italian natural philosopher Bernardino Telesio[19] to Marin Cureau de La Chambre[20] and Scipio Chiaramonti (who cites La Chambre on the soul along with Aristotle's *Rhetoric*); from Lutheran Aristotelians of mid-century Helmstedt such as Hermann Conring (who edited Chiaramonti's *Passions of the Soul*)[21] to polyhistorian Daniel Georg Morhof (who cites Chiaramonti and Aristotle in his review of literature on "erudite conversation");[22] from a now obscure mayor of Frankfurt/O.

19. Telesio treats the passions in typically Aristotelian fashion: passions are identified according to the opposing virtues and vices they generate (a schematic drawn from Aristotle's *Rhetoric*), and then Aristotle's critical transition from book 1 to book 2 of the *Nicomachean Ethics* is cited at length—the passage in which Aristotle argues that virtues both intellectual and moral are a matter of good habit (*ethos*). Bernardinus Telesius, *De rerum natura iuxta propria principia libri IX* (Naples: Salviano, 1586; reprint, Hildesheim: Olms, 1971), 359–400.

20. Marin Cureau de La Chambre, *Le systeme de l'âme* (Paris: d'Allin, 1665).

21. Scipione Chiaramonti (Scipio Claramontius), *De coniectandis cuiusque moribus et latitantibus animi affectibus libri decem; Opus novi argumenti et incomparabile, cura H. Conringii recensitum* (Helmstedt: Müller, 1665).

22. "De conversatione erudita," "Homiletices eruditae." Daniel Georg Morhof, *Polyhistor literarius philosophicus*, rev. ed. (Lubeck: Böckmann, 1714). Morhof suggests that civil prudence requires attention to mores and affects, and the authors he recommends on the topic include Aristotle (*Rhetoric*, book 2), Chiaramonti, and Camillus

and University Professor Arnold Wesenfeld[23] to famed Conring student and philosopher of the early Enlightenment Wilhelm Gottfried Leibniz.[24] What these authors share besides a loose scholarly genealogy is a fascination with corporeal dynamics on the Aristotelian, and not the Cartesian, model. Whether praised or blamed, the "irrational" soul was seen by all as the source of human motivation, and all (besides Leibniz) sought to devise a science that would institutionalize irrational power for the common good. When it came to harnessing the passions, Aristotle was *the* authority. A moral philosophy of the passions was drawn from the *Nicomachean Ethics*, and a pragmatic phenomenology of the passions from Aristotle's *Rhetoric*.

In the *Rhetoric*, Aristotle explains first that passions condition our very ability to evaluate the world. "The emotions [*pathe*] are those things through which, by undergoing change, people come to differ in their judgments and which are accompanied by pain and pleasure, for example, anger, pity, fear, and other such things and their opposites (1378a21)." Fear, for instance, is a reaction to potential suffering that makes people "inclined to deliberation"

Baldus, *Physionomica Aristotelis* and *De propensionibus hominum* (151). In his compact history of rhetoric, Morhof emphasizes pathology and the rhetoric of persuasion, praising in nonsectarian fashion Jesuit authors, including Caussin (941).

23. Arnold Wesenfeld (d. 1727) was a professor of logic, ethics, and metaphysics at Frankfurt/O. His relevant books include *Dissertatio de natura definitionis*; *Georgica animae et vitae*; *Passiones animi*; and *Versuch einer Verbesserung der Moral unter den Christen*.

24. Leibniz thought untenable Samuel Pufendorf's "new scientific" distinction between internal and external actions designed to subvert Aristotelian teleology. If human jurisdiction were limited to external actions, Leibniz argued, we would lose access as human scientists to the very teleological dispositions that cause people to act in particular ways. Leibniz was quick to point out that virtuous behavior, such as self-sacrifice for a loved one, is a matter of dispositional *mores*, not law: "Therefore he who has control of the education and instruction of others is obligated, by natural law, to form minds with eminent precepts, and to take care that the practice of virtue, almost like a second nature, guides the will toward the good. This is the most trustworthy method of education because, according to Aristotle's fine saying, customs [*mores*] are stronger than laws." Gottfried Wilhelm Leibniz, "Opinion on the Principles of Pufendorf" (1706), in *Leibniz: Political Writings*, ed. and trans. Patrick Riley (Cambridge: Cambridge University Press, 1972), 69.

(1383a7). "How might we avoid this threat?" the statesman might ask. Aristotle then explains that the passions are basic social phenomena, best treated by asking three questions: "I mean, for example, in speaking of anger, what is their *state of mind* when people are angry and against *whom* are they usually angry, and for what sort of *reasons*" (1378a25–26). We can get a good sense of passion's social constitution by looking at just one portion of Aristotle's acute treatment of shame (*aiskhyne*).

> Since shame is imagination [*phantasia*] about a loss of reputation and for its own sake, not for its results, and since no one cares about reputation [in the abstract] but on account of those who hold an opinion of him, necessarily a person feels shame toward those whose opinion he takes account of. He takes account of those who admire him and whom he admires and by whom he wishes to be admired and those to whose rank he aspires and those whose opinion he does not despise. Now people want to be admired by those and admire those who have something good in the way of honors or from whom they happen to be greatly in need of something those people have in their control, as lovers [want love or sexual favors]; but they aspire to the rank of those [they regard as] like themselves, and they take account of prudent people as telling the truth, and their elders and educated people are of such a sort. And they feel more shame at things done before these people's eyes and in the open; hence, too the proverb "Shame is in the eyes." (1384a22–36)

Any illusion we might have that passions can best be understood as psychophysiological sufferings of the individual is thereby laid to rest: shame as Aristotle describes it is irreducibly social. Moreover, a review of the second book of Aristotle's *Rhetoric* reveals that social difference even determines what a neurobiologist of emotion such as Antonio Damasio would call the "primary emotions," such as fear and joy, just as it does a "secondary emotion," such as shame. For Aristotle it would be untenable to distinguish in this way between emotions that are socially constituted and those that are not.

Certainly someone who feels shame might turn beet red, but to limit one's analysis of shame to its physics as Descartes and

Damasio do is, to put it mildly, a bit thin. For the causes of shame, according to Aristotle, are directly related to a person's position in any given social situation and the stock in that position he or she holds. Shame is a complex phenomenon with a series of subtle enabling conditions: there can be no shame where there is no reputation to lose (a *faux pas* among strangers), where a loss of reputation is not recognized (one is unaware of the error), where its loss is merely imagined (stumbling with no one to see it), or where its loss has no repercussions (among socially independent inferiors). Conversely, there *is* shame where social institutions are most dense: where one's reputation really matters, where the opinions of others are valued, where social rank is effective, where credit can be given and debts owed, where honor can be realized or lost, where there are fragile bonds of intimacy, and where social prestige can be measured according to one's institutional access to the truth (for example, through formal education, demonstrated credibility).

We should thus be able to see most clearly how passions are inequitably distributed, exchanged, and monopolized where social difference is most extreme. A slave, for instance, does not provoke in a master passions such as friendly feeling, confidence, or even pity, because, according to Aristotle, pity is directed toward those of equal status who have suffered a wrong unjustly. An equal, and not an inferior, represents the possibility that one might similarly suffer without cause. Therefore, Aristotle does not mention slaves directly in his discussion of shame, since doing something dishonorable in front of someone without status carries no direct consequences. Nonetheless, Aristotle warns that the relationship with a slave can be a source of shame because it is never known to whom the slave will reveal the master's dishonor. A slave is thus a vehicle of emotion, but not an origin or end.

Of course, for Aristotle, the politician would not be concerned with a mere "patient" of passion such as a woman, a child, or a slave. Instead, the politician's job is to address those capable of political agency by invoking social institutions that embody beneficial passions—such as anger well directed (*orge*), calmness (*praotes*), confidence (*tharsos*), emulation (*zelos*), as well as shame—evoking in a speech, for instance, a political scenario in which the imagined shameful consequences of a contemplated action serve as deterrent. In this regard, Aristotle provides a helpful example. After capturing the island of Samos, Athenians debated sending settlers there in violation of the intent of the Second Athenian League of 377/376. Cydias asks those engaged in a debate about allotment of land to "imagine [all] the Greeks standing around them in a circle, actually seeing and not only later hearing about what they might vote" (1384b32–35). In this case, the statesman invokes the figure of a tribunal of conscience in order to evoke shame among those whose reputation is potentially threatened—and this to help an assembly reach a decision compatible with the law. The more stable these social institutions and the more heavily citizens are invested in the community, the more rhetorical capital the politician will then have to work with. Finally, we learn from Aristotle's discussion of shame that rhetorical capital takes the form of a double-sided emotional/verbal currency—the value of which is a function of the social milieu through which it flows.

Hobbes and the Political Economy of Emotion

"Fear makes people inclined to deliberation." This is Aristotle's succinct formulation of a philosophical claim even more far-reaching: reason is grounded in passion.[25] But it is Thomas Hobbes, perennial friend of the powers that be and witness to the brutal English Civil War, who would follow the implications of this Aristotelian position to its practical conclusion, finally building an expansive political science upon it in the form of

---

25. This interpretation of Aristotle is fleshed out in Gross and Kemmann, *Heidegger and Rhetoric* (see introduction, n. 15).

the *Leviathan*. Beginning in classic Aristotelian fashion, Hobbes writes the following "Of Man":

> When in the mind of man, Appetites, and Aversions, Hopes, and Feares, concerning one and the same thing, arise alternately; and divers goods and evill consequences of the doing, or omitting the thing propounded, come successively into our thoughts; so that sometimes we have an Appetite to it; sometimes an Aversion from it; sometimes Hope to be able to do it; sometimes Despaire, or Feare to attempt it; the whole summe of Desires, Aversions, Hopes and Fears, continued till the thing will be either done, or thought impossible, is that we call DELIBERATION. (44)

But here we must take careful note. The scenario Hobbes describes is not the familiar one in which we are attracted or repelled, encouraged or threatened, and *then*—as a result of our uncomfortable emotional state—appeal to reason for assistance. Instead, that exercise of reason that we call "deliberation" is composed *precisely* of "the whole summe of Desires, Aversions, Hopes and Fears" drawn to a logical conclusion. Indeed, to be without passion is, for Hobbes, to be without "wit" altogether (and here Damasio would certainly agree). For a person who has no great passion "is as men terme it indifferent; though he may be so farre a good man, as to be free from giving offence; yet he cannot possibly have either a great Fancy, or much Judgement" (*Leviathan*, 53).

In his treatment of felicity, Hobbes in fact takes a direct shot at a Stoic philosophy that would extirpate the passions, preferring instead the framework of Aristotelian physics (modified to a degree by Galileo's and Harvey's new science of motion). "*Continuall successe* in obtaining those things which a man from time to time desireth, that is to say, continuall prospering, is that men call FELICITY; I mean the Felicity of this life. For there is no such thing as perpetuall Tranquility of mind, while we live here; because Life it selfe is but Motion, and can never be without Desire, nor without Feare, no more than without Sense" (*Leviathan*, 46). Indeed, the very notion that language could be drained of emotion and distilled into the form of pure reason (as Samuel Pufendorf would later imagine) is summarily dismissed by Hobbes. Moral philosophy entails for Hobbes not the discernment of absolute moral imperatives under the dim glow of a *lumen naturale*, but a project constitutive of social difference. "Morall Philosophy," Hobbes remarks, "is nothing else but the Science of what is *Good*, and *Evill*, in the conversation, and Society of man-kind." Good and evil, Hobbes continues, "are names that signifie our Appetites, and Aversions [i.e., passions]; which in different tempers, customes, and doctrines of men, are different" (*Leviathan*, 110).

Passions in the Hobbesian world are thus anterior to and constitutive of political agency, though they are by no means biological givens. An emotion such as jealousy originates not from within—not in the biological organism jealous of scarce resources, for instance—but rather is constituted without, in the contested space *between* politically and historically situated agents. Indeed, a Hobbesian commonwealth in which every member enjoyed equal status would be completely devoid of passion. And as Hobbes emphasizes in each of his treatments of politics from *Elements of Law* to *Behemoth*, it is social difference in its purest form, or vainglory, that names the uniquely human vulnerability at the origin of civil society.

That humans are "by nature equall" in both body and intellect is tragically distorted by our first-person perspective, for as Hobbes neatly observes in the *Leviathan*, men inescapably "see their own wit at hand, and other mens at a distance" (*Leviathan*, 86–87). And insofar as sense perception in all cases is "nothing els but originall fancy" detached from the things themselves (*Leviathan*, 14), humans are inherently vulnerable to perceptual errors both at the lower order of optics and at the higher order of social relations. Indeed, the fundamental distortion in social relations Hobbes calls "vainglory" precedes even the passions of love and fear in the process that eventually produces civil society. But as we see in Hobbes's condemnation of romance in general and the "gallant madness" of Don Quixote in particular,[26] vainglory is most dangerous where eloquence and social imagination is most developed. Such was the case, for instance, in the seditious Long Parliament, where, according to Hobbes, arrogant Presbyterian ministers jealous of the authority of bishops used fiery rhetoric and loose interpretation of scripture to provoke their more moderate parliamentary colleagues into open rebellion.[27]

Since by definition there is never enough glory to go around, *vain*glory is built into the very fabric of society. Thus, opposed to the philosophers of the Scottish Enlightenment, such as Francis Hutcheson and Adam Smith, who later tried to anchor social passions in a moral sense equally shared by all, Hobbes follows Aristotle in sketching an economy of emotional scarcity, a zero-sum game where the emotional wealth of one social agent necessarily comes at the expense of another.[28] Compounding this human tragedy for Hobbes is the fact that human beings are by nature provided the "multiplying glasses" that distort social relations, whereas they naturally lack the "prospective glasses" that would correct them: namely, moral and civil science. Hobbes sees it precisely as his task in the *Leviathan* to provide the unnatural science that would correct social passions toward adequate civil obedience (*Leviathan*, 129). Passions for Hobbes will always be unfairly distributed, but at least moral and civil science can help us manage how inequity can be mobilized for the sake of peace.

>>><<<

Though Hobbes famously complains to John Aubrey that Aristotle was the worst teacher of politics and ethics there had ever been, he concedes that Aristotle's discourses of animals and

26. Thomas Hobbes, *De corpore politico* (England: Thoemmes Press, 1994), 58.

27. Thomas Hobbes, *Behemoth: The History of the Causes of the Civil Wars of England, and of the Counsels and Artifices by Which They Were Carried on from the Year 1640 to the Years 1660*, ed. William Molesworth, Ben Franklin Research and Source Works Series no. 38 (New York: B. Franklin, 1963), 30, 36, 66, 136.

28. Thomas Hobbes, *De cive* (English), ed. Howard Warrender (Oxford: Clarendon Press, 1983), 44.

rhetoric were "rare."[29] So rare, in fact, that Hobbes takes the time early in his career to translate in digest form Aristotle's *Rhetoric* for his young charge the third Earl of Devonshire. No doubt Hobbes found the scholastic Aristotle objectionable, but as Leo Strauss convincingly demonstrated decades ago, the humanistic Aristotle—and particularly the Aristotle of the *Rhetoric*, book 2— had a profound and lasting impact on Hobbes's mature political theory, despite scholarly claims to the contrary that *Leviathan* is essentially the natural science of Galileo and Descartes applied to people.[30] In fact, Aristotle's subtle imbrication of human emotions and human institutions made his rhetorical theory appealing to all sorts of early modern political theorists either unaware of or unconvinced by the new psychophysiology of Descartes. This includes Descartes's hostile correspondent Hobbes, a figure frequently mischaracterized since at least C. B. MacPherson as a natural scientist of the body politic and a prophet of competitive individualism.

Though Hobbes does indeed characterize the state of nature as the fearful war "of every man, against every man" (*Leviathan*, 88), his theory of the passions shows that he was much more than a protoliberal with a taste for mechanical explanations. If anything, it would be more accurate to describe Hobbes as a

29. John Aubrey, *"Brief Lives," chiefly of Contemporaries, set down by John Aubrey, between the Years 1669 & 1696*, ed. Andrew Clark (Oxford: Clarendon, 1898), 357. I thank Nancy Struever for alerting me to this passage.

30. Leo Strauss, *The Political Philosophy of Hobbes: Its Basis in Genesis*, trans. Elsa M. Sinclair (Chicago: University of Chicago Press, 1952); C. B. MacPherson, *The Political Theory of Possessive Individualism: Hobbes to Locke* (Oxford: Clarendon Press, 1962). See also David Johnston, *The Rhetoric of* Leviathan: *Thomas Hobbes and the Politics of Cultural Transformation* (Princeton, NJ: Princeton University Press, 1986); Victoria Kahn, "Hobbes, Romance, and the Contract of Mimesis," *Political Theory* 29, no. 1 (2001): 4–29; Richard Tuck, "Hobbes and Descartes," in *Perspectives on Thomas Hobbes*, ed. G. A. J. Rogers and Alan Ryan (Oxford: Oxford University Press, 1988); Richard Tuck, "Hobbes's Moral Philosophy," in *The Cambridge Companion to Hobbes*, ed. Tom Sorell (Cambridge: Cambridge University Press, 1996). On passions as social difference in Hobbes, see Paul Dumouchel, *Émotions: Essai sur le corps et le social* (Paris: Synthélabo, 1995); for a counterview, see Tom Sorell, "Hobbes's UnAristotelian Political Rhetoric," *Philosophy and Rhetoric* 23, no. 2 (1990): 96–108.

protocommunitarian insofar as he was concerned with social passions that incline humans to war, such as indignation, covetous-
ness, jealousy, vengefulness, vainglory, dejection, impudence, and
cruelty; and those equally social passions that incline humans to
peace, such as anxiety, hope, benevolence, magnanimity, kindness, admiration, pity, and shame (*Leviathan*, chap. 6). The trick
for Hobbes was not to extirpate the passions in Stoic fashion, for
this would leave behind not a rational subject inclined to good
judgment, but an apathetic dullard. Rather, for Hobbes as for
Aristotle, the goal was to determine the best way to articulate
political institutions that embody more benign passions.

Following Aristotle, passions did not have to be treated as
regrettable mental errors per Galen or Seneca. Nor did passions have to be treated taxonomically, whether in the form of a
simplistic rhetorical handbook or a treatise designed to classify
facial expressions (such as those written by Charles Le Brun and
Johann-Caspar Lavater—the father of the nineteenth-century
science of physiognomy and forerunner of Darwin and Ekman).[31]
Nor did passions have to be understood as the external expression
of an internal state, as Romantics would later maintain. Instead,
pathos in Hobbes's scheme could be related in complex fashion
to both logos and ethos—both social discourse and habits of the
soul. Passions demanded a specific social context and appropriate
narrative if they were to be rightly represented or, perhaps better
said, effectively put into play. For an important set of early modern political theorists, including Hobbes, the task was to apply
Aristotle's rhetorical theory of the passions even more rigorously
to the political body, while integrating into the analysis a new
relativity of temperament that was thought to extend to human
nature itself.

31. Le Brun, *Method to Learn* (see chap. 1, n. 3); Johann-Caspar Lavater, *Physiog-
nomische Fragmente, zur Beförderung der Menschenkenntniss und Menschenliebe* (Leipzig:
Weidmanns Erben und Reich, 1775–1778); *Physiognomy; or, The Corresponding Analogy
between the Conformation of the Features and the Ruling Passions of the Mind* (London:
Printed for H. D. Symonds, 1790).

However, as Aristotle's treatment of the master/slave relationship and Hobbes's treatment of vainglory have shown, it matters not only where passions are invested, but also where they are denied. The positive function of passions depends upon an economy of scarcity characterized by carefully cultivated apathy.[32] That is to say, it makes a difference in the end not only what sort of passions are distributed to whom, but also how they are hoarded and monopolized and how their systematic denial helps produce political subjects of a certain kind. And when we consider the political economy of passions in the culture of mid-seventeenth-century England or even today, we should be able to account both for those who would cultivate apathy as an antidote to public distress and those who are marginalized precisely by their exclusion from passions such as pride, anger, and pity. In fact, in an age such as ours, challenged once again by political apathy and the specter of zero-sum pluralism, the passionate pessimism of Thomas Hobbes seems particularly instructive.

Indeed, it will be my contention in the chapters that follow that this early modern, rhetorical understanding of emotion is indispensable in our efforts to negotiate emotions in our own late-modern situations: to recognize how apathy is a carefully

32. Political apathy had widespread currency during the Civil War that so preoccupied Hobbes and his contemporaries. Besides looking to the Stoic tradition, quietism, and the emerging campaign against religious enthusiasm, those eager for a political settlement that would judiciously withdraw passion from the public sphere might invoke the famous Pauline injunction from Romans 13.1 endorsed by Calvin: "Let every person be in subjection to the governing authorities. For there is no authority except from God, and those which exist are established by God." Quentin Skinner, for one, has argued that there was a secular version of this attitude reflected in the obsession of Royalist poets with the innocent pleasures of pastoral retreat (think of Edmund Waller, Abraham Cowley, Izaak Walton, and Henry Vaughan). According to Skinner, pastoral is implicated in Civil War politics precisely by virtue of its idyllic shepherds whose private passion is carefully staged *outside* of class and public life. Quentin Skinner, "Conquest and Consent: Thomas Hobbes and the Engagement Controversy," in *The Interregnum: The Quest for Settlement 1646–1660*, ed. G. E. Aylmer (London: Archon, 1972), 79–98; see also his *Reason and Rhetoric in the Philosophy of Hobbes* (Cambridge: Cambridge University Press, 1996).

cultivated political category (chapter 2), how passivity serves as a precondition for political activism (chapter 3), how the passion of humility constitutes a positive form of the self (chapter 4), and finally how, generally speaking, psyche is a matter of social difference (chapter 5). Reaching behind the scientific understanding of emotion that runs from Descartes to Damasio and again focusing upon the rhetoric and politics of emotion gives us a sophisticated framework to talk about emotion beyond what can be revealed in a face or in a theory of evolutionary biology. Emotion's uneven expression over different sorts of people, its apparent dysfunction in the humiliated or depressed, or even its utter absence in the politically disaffected must be understood as meaningful beyond Damasio's pathologies of the psychological individual or Ekman's "display rules" that explain expressive differences across cultures. Only then might systemic emotional problems be addressed with anything more than the latest version of a metaphorical or actual antidepressant.

2

Apathy in the Shadow Economy of Emotion

We put down mad dogs; we kill the wild, untamed ox; we use the knife on sick sheep to stop their infecting the flock; we destroy abnormal offspring at birth; children, too, if they are born weak or deformed, we drown. Yet this is not the work of anger, but of reason—to separate the sound from the worthless.
«SENECA, *On Anger*»

The *a* in apathy suggests a profound personal deficiency, a passionless condition fully detached from the cares and responsibilities of the world. Indeed, apathy—along with its relatives acedia, melancholy, indifference, boredom, ennui, and "spleen"—has been considered at least since Augustine a condition of moral depravity, a defiant retreat from the world of God and humankind.[1] But much can be gained, I wager, if we consider apathy something

1. For Augustine's objection to Stoic apathy, see *The City of God against the Pagans*, 9.4–5. Though tangential to my argument here, a comparison of seventeenth-century apathy and eighteenth-century boredom is illuminating. Whereas apathy speaks to the tension between human nature and the supernatural or preternatural, boredom in its definitive Johnsonian version is a kind of internal, psychic tension. Boredom is manifest in a new relationship to time and emerges along with the new class phenomenon of leisure: now time can be "wasted" or "spent" wisely. See Samuel Johnson, *The Idler*, ed. W. J. Bate, John M. Bullitt, and L. F. Powell (New Haven, CT: Yale University Press, 1963), esp. 46–48, 50. See also Patricia Meyer Spacks, *Boredom: The Literary History*

more than the zero degree in the scale of human emotion. Though our scientific and postromantic cultures can make this difficult to see, apathy is productive, and it is also produced, with great social effort. One goal of this second chapter is to cultivate by way of critical intellectual history our ability to see how apathy shapes public life.

The English word *apathy* is related to the Greek *apatheia*, which means, literally, without passion-as-suffering. It is typically translated into Latin by the Stoic philosopher Seneca and others as *impassibilitas*.[2] Thus, if passion, and therefore apathy, is to be rightly understood, it is first helpful to get our minds around the classical understanding of suffering. One way to do this is to divorce suffering from its implication that pain is primarily what one suffers. In fact, the semantics of classical Greek and Latin allows one to "suffer," or simply to undergo, pleasure, for instance. To suffer a passion, then, need not be an unpleasant experience. But we should also seriously consider the implication in the epigram above that suffering an emotion might be by nature pathological, an unhappy deviation from the norm of reason. This association has an equally distinguished lineage, captured in the Ciceronian Stoic understanding of emotion as *perturbationes animi*: a deviation from reason and an illness of the soul.[3] On this understanding, apathy would indeed be desirable, for it would designate a state of tranquility amenable to reason. My contention is that neither of these philological alternatives, or even both together, adequately captures the phenomenon. And the inadequacy is meaningful. Passions and their evaluation, and thus apathy and its evaluation, vary dramatically from one practical situation to the next, and only a critical intellectual history can give adequate meaning to this variation. Hence, a guiding

---

of a State of Mind (Chicago: University of Chicago Press, 1995). For a discussion of melancholia, see chapter 4 below.

2. For Seneca references in chapter 2, refer to John M. Cooper and J. F. Procopé, eds., *Seneca: Moral and Political Essays* (Cambridge: Cambridge University Press, 1995).

3. Cicero, *Tusculan Disputations*, 3.7.

historical question: what do we learn about apathy in our late-modern political culture by figuring out why it was endorsed by Roman and early modern Stoics? Under what historical conditions, in other words, can we consider apathy a productive force in shaping public life?[4]

Methodologically, I am interested in how the explicit argument for or against the passions is cast and what textual strategies allow the explicit argument to function. For instance, we can read Seneca's explicit argument about universal human nature and the "unnaturalness" of the passions while asking the questions Who is speaking? To whom? What would be the advantage of apathy given the immediate circumstances? How does the argument characterize different sorts of relationships between people? By what mechanism are the characteristics of human nature identified by Seneca unevenly distributed across monarchs, aristocrats, soldiers, noncitizens of Rome, women, children, and slaves?

Finally, in this chapter I consider why apathy does not fit comfortably into a scientific model of emotional universalism and expression, even when explained by Paul Ekman's "display rules" whereby the apparently stoic countenance of Japanese, for instance, can be dismissed as a cultural mask superimposed upon the emotional truth of a human nature equally shared by all.[5]

---

4. This critical perspective reveals a puzzle at the heart of our own political culture: in order to realize our potential as modern citizen-subjects while avoiding something like Nazi irrationalism, we are encouraged to be rational (i.e., unemotional) about politics, but not apathetic. Of course this position is contradictory on the surface, and it indicates a host of problems, from political disaffection to our difficulty accounting for ethnic communities with conflicting affective histories. For a sophisticated discussion of the contradictions inherent in contemporary political disaffection, see Nina Eliasoph, *Avoiding Politics: How Americans Produce Apathy in Everyday Life* (Cambridge: Cambridge University Press, 1998). Eliasoph, in her sociological analysis of the evaporation of politics in the U.S. public sphere, remarks that "simple apathy" never explained the political silence she heard while studying her subjects in the Buffalo, New York, community. "Inside of 'apathy' was a whole underwater world of denials, omissions, evasions, things forgotten, skirted, avoided, and suppressed—a world as varied and colorful as a tropical undersea bed" (255). My work in this chapter is designed, in part, to explain how *apathy* became such a vexed term.

5. For a popular account, see Ekman, *Emotions Revealed*, 4 (see introduction, n. 2).

Apathy provides a key example of how the rhetorical analysis of emotion gives us access to phenomena obscured by brain science or any other mode of analysis that depends centrally upon biophysiology or some strong notion of a psychological individual. Brain scientists and scientific psychologists just aren't interested in apathy per se, beyond its very distant and very modern cousins such as depression. What, after all, does a brain scan of apathy look like? Where in the brain is apathy located? How might it be measured and treated? States of psychological tranquility or depression can be measured against relative brain activity, and they frequently are, with therapeutic implications. Both science and everyday usage tells us, however, that tranquility and depression are not the same thing as apathy, which is a term typically left in the purview of the social sciences.[6]

Though it will be useful to map manifest emotions onto particular forms of the early modern psyche—showing, for instance, in chapter 4 how English laws of patrilineal inheritance materialized the inequality of pride and humility across gender—apathy best reveals in its "absence" the general structure of emotional economies. For in the *a* that signifies a marked nonpresence of emotion, we intuitively read not an arithmetic zero point but rather a node of special density in a dynamic social field, where the very possibility of emotion is at issue. In this chapter, I push

6. Consider, for instance, the familiar "voter apathy" discussed by columnist John Nichols in an October 1998 *Progressive* article entitled "Apathy, Inc." Invoking abortion clinic terrorist Randall Terry's prayer for a low turnout as he ran for Congress in a competitive upstate New York district, Nichols documents how Republican operatives think strategically about political inertia. "Politics is about two things," Republican pollster Bill McInturff is reported to say: "mobilizing your voters, and not mobilizing the other side." The strategy for conservatives is to "reduce the juice" or to lower the interest in political participation to such an extent that "the small percentage of voters who zealously back conservative causes can dominate." To this end, Nichols goes on to explain, adult men and women are being tested by the nation's top political consultants—hooked up to monitoring devices that measure "surges and downturns in their pulse rates" as they view videotapes of candidates delivering speeches, mock newscasts, and television commercials extolling or defaming particular politicians.

the social analysis of emotion one more step in the direction of the humanities by considering apathy not just as the absence of emotion, but rather as the rhetorically constituted shadow economy against which a positive economy of emotion is fashioned.

Reason versus Passion: Early Modern Topoi

Scanning the entry for *Affecten* in Christoph Lehmann's widely read German lexicon of adages (1639), we see an overgrowth of Neostoicisms that point unmistakably toward the Age of Reason in its cartoon form. "The passions reside in the belly, reason in the brain, yet inferior rules superior." "Passions are like enemies ... that must be attacked as soon as they set foot in one's land." "It is easier to shut out the passions than to rule them." "When one has the smoke of passions in one's head, reason becomes clouded." "As are the passions, so is the matter at hand—from molehills are made mountains, from mountains molehills." "He who hangs on the passions loses grip on the truth, mixing up right and wrong." "A wise and God-fearing man rules the stars, and so he can master the passions with God's help, prayer, and moderation."[7] Indeed, when we review the so-called political literature of the German Baroque—from Daniel Lohenstein's plays[8] to Christian Georg von Bessel's *Neuer Politischer Glücks=Schmied*,[9] from Christian Weise's massive *Politischer*

---

7. Christoph Lehmann, *Florilegium Politicum: Politischer Blumen Garten / Darinn Außerlesene Sententz / Lehren / Regulen und Sprüchwörter Aus Theologis, Jurisconsultis, Politicis, Historicis, Philosophis, Poëten, und eigener erfahrung unter 286. Tituln / zu sondern nutzen und Lust Hohen und Niedern im Reden / Rahten und Schreiben / das gut zubrauchen und das böß zu meiden. In locos communes zusammen getragen* (Lübeck: Jungen, 1639; reprint, Bern: Lang, 1986), 2–6.

8. On Lohenstein and the political man in the seventeenth century, see Karl-Heinz Mulagk, *Phänomene des politischen Menschen im 17. Jahrhundert: Propädeutische Studien zum Werk Lohensteins unter besonderer Berücksichtigung Diego Saavedra Fajardos und Baltasar Graciáns* (Berlin: Schmidt, 1973).

9. Christian Georg von Bessel, *Neuer Politischer Glücks=Schmied / Mit allerhand Zum Hof= und Welt=Leben dienenden / und auff gegenwärtige Zeiten absonderlich gerichteten heylsamen und höchstnöthigen Lehren ...* (Frankfurt: Naumann, 1681).

Redner[10] to Christoph Lehmann's *Florilegium Politicum*—the evidence clearly shows that "prudence" in seventeenth-century political culture was underwritten by Stoic philosophy and thus came at the expense of free-ranging human passions, those "accidental" movements of the soul that cloud good judgment and cause devastating political blindness.[11] Evident as well in the monumental midcentury treatises on natural law, Stoic teachings had important consequences for more

10. For Weise, the health of the political body (*politische Körper*) depends upon correctly identifying the causes of political illness (*politische Kranckheit*). And political illness turns out to be caused by excesses of passion manifest precisely when a political subject exceeds the bounds of normal "curiosity"—acts out, so to speak—and unsettles the entire organism. Weise, *Politischer Redner* (see introduction, n. 14). For commentary on Weise, see Gotthardt Frühsorge's *Der politische Körper: Zum Begriff des Politischen im 17. Jahrhundert und in den Romanen Christian Weises* (Stuttgart: Metzler, 1974). Frühsorge builds upon Dilthey's research by arguing that the Neostoic theory of passions (promoted also by Dutch philologists Daniel Heinsius, Gerhard Johann Vossius, and Caspar Scioppius), provides the background against which one can make sense of the truly odd function of the term *politics* in seventeenth-century German court literature.

11. A classic in the genre is Justus Lipsius, *Von der Bestendigkeit* [De constantia], trans. Andreas Viritus (1599), ed. Leonard Forster (Stuttgart: Metzler, 1965). For commentary, see Gerhard Oestreich, *Neostoicism and the Early Modern State*, ed. Brigitta Oestreich and H. G. Koenigsberger, trans. David McLintock (Cambridge: Cambridge University Press, 1982). Wilhelm Dilthey's influential studies on the topic include "Die Funktion der Anthropologie in der Kultur des 16. und 17. Jahrhunderts," in *Weltanschauung und Analyse des Menschen Seit Renaissance und Reformation*, vol. 2 of *Wilhelm Diltheys Gesammelte Schriften* (Leipzig: Teubner, 1914); "Auffassung un Analyse des Menschen im 15. und 16. Jahrhundert," and "Das natürliche System der Geisteswissenschaften im 17. Jahrhundert," in *Aufsätze zur Philosophie*, ed. Marion Marquardt (Berlin: Dausien, 1986). Consider also Reinhart Koselleck's important thesis regarding the relative scope of politics. Conscience, Koselleck argues, was a casualty of the devastating religious wars that ravaged Europe through the first half of the seventeenth century, driven from the political stage in the effort to establish political authority immune to the factionalization of belief. In place of a conscience manifest in the public realm grew the absolute power of the sovereign to make decisions, and this even in Germany, where sovereign power was manifest in fractious territorial states. So to the extent that access to the traditional political realm shrank, so grew the political significance of social, cultural, and moral realms. These realms were populated, according to Koselleck, by social institutions such as the French Freemasons and the German *Illuminati*. Koselleck's formula is: "Conscience, which becomes alienated from the State, turns into private morality." See Reinhart Koselleck, *Critique and Crisis: Enlightenment and the Pathogenesis of Modern Society* (Oxford: Berg, 1988), 31.

serious political thought across the European continent and in England. Citing Seneca's *On Benefits*, the Dutch political theorist Hugo Grotius famously set "natural reason" against the passions in the fashion typical of Stoic moral philosophy. He writes in his masterwork, *De jure belli ac pacis libri tres* (1625):

> Since over other animals man has advantage of possessing not only a strong bent towards social life . . . but also a power of discrimination which enables him to decide what things are agreeable or harmful (as to both things present and things to come), and what can lead to either alternative: in such things it is meet for the nature of man, within the limitations of human intelligence, to follow the direction of a well-tempered judgment, being neither led astray by fear or the allurement of immediate pleasure, nor carried away by rash impulse. Whatever is clearly at variance with such judgment is understood to be contrary also to the law of nature, that is, to the nature of man.[12]

But in a manner fitting for a subtle thinker in this age that saw the tension between natural science and religion intensify, Grotius the good Christian is, in fact, equivocal on this point of passion. He slavishly promotes neither the radical purging of passion by reason, nor a simplified Aristotelian/Peripatetic doctrine of the Mean. For to do so would be in some cases a display of failing virtue:

> the truth is that some virtues do tend to keep passions under control; but that is not because such control is a proper and essential characteristic of every virtue. Rather it is because right reason, which virtue everywhere follows, in some things prescribes the pursuing of a middle course, in others stimulates to the utmost degree. We cannot, for example, worship God too much; for superstition errs not by worshipping God too much, but by worshipping in a perverse way. Neither can we too much seek after the blessings that shall abide for ever, nor fear too much the everlasting evils, nor have too great hatred for sin. (25–26)

12. Hugo Grotius, *On the Laws of War and Peace*, vol. 2, ed. F. W. Kelsey, A. E. R. Boak, H. A. Sanders, and J. S. Reeves, trans. Francis W. Kelsey (Oxford: Clarendon, 1925), 13.

Here Grotius pays tribute to the Christian Aristotelian valuation of the passions while cleverly maintaining his rational stance: loving God and hating sin is ultimately a matter of right reason.

Samuel Pufendorf's theory of natural law is less subtle. Rejecting the "Epicurianism" of Hobbes, while claiming the heritage of Stoic "dignity and tranquillity,"[13] this first political theorist of the Westphalian era was determined to build his system upon pure reason rather than the passions that seemed to have fueled the religious wars of the preceding century. His solution is as famous as it is influential. Citing Seneca's *On Anger*, Pufendorf draws a radical distinction between internal life governed by moral theology and external life governed by natural law: "human jurisdiction is concerned only with a man's external actions and does not penetrate to what is hidden in the heart and which gives no external effect or sign, and consequently takes no account of it" (9). No doubt this passage from Pufendorf's *De officio hominis et civis* seems reasonable enough to those of us who assume the virtues of contractarian philosophy, freedom of thought, and the division of church and state. However, drawing this radical distinction between internal and external life requires that we pay a price in terms of our liberal sensibilities, for Stoic political pathology promotes a kind of absolutism that extends even to the way people are supposed to speak. Just as individuals have particular temperaments, habits, and passions, so do "whole nations." And just as individuals can do a good deal to blunt the edge of their temperaments, curb bad habits, and check their passions before they issue in action, so should sovereigns govern their political bodies. For the ideal state is one of "rest in quiet and tranquillity" rather than one "shaken by the peculiar motions which we call passions" (20–21). Maintaining corporate health thus means for Pufendorf enforcing corporate peace of mind: "The internal

13. Samuel Pufendorf, *On the Duty of Man and Citizen*, ed. James Tully, trans. Michael Silverthorne (Cambridge: Cambridge University Press, 1991), xxvii–xxviii. This work is a compendium of Pufendorf's magnum opus, *De iure naturae et gentium libri octo*; *On the Law of Nature and Nations*, 2 vols., trans. C. H. Oldfather and W. A. Oldfather, Classics of International Law (Oxford: Clarendon, 1934).

health and stability of states results from the union of the citizens, and the more perfect it is, the more effectively the force of government will pervade the whole body of the state." Therefore, Pufendorf concludes ominously, it is the sovereign's task both to prevent citizens from forming associations by private agreements and "to ensure that factions do not arise" (154).

The Stoic association of pathos with harmful perturbation, however, has never gone unchallenged. The Stoic view must be contrasted both with Aristotle's view and with the later Christian Aristotelianism that infused early modern political thought. For Christian Aristotelians, hostility to the phenomenal world was manifest not in a passionless existence outside, but rather in what Erich Auerbach once described as a "counter-suffering" within the world. According to early and medieval Christian authors such as Bonaventure, it is only the passion of love that can lead through suffering to *excessus mentis* and union with Christ.[14] Indeed, a Lutheran natural and social science developed by Philipp Melanchthon that maintained a strong presence through the German Baroque and beyond was pointedly *anti*-Stoic, and later anti-Cartesian as well, for some of the same reasons.[15] Rather than accidents of natural integrity, passions

14. "In this sense the *passiones* remain something which the soul suffers, by which it is assailed—and in this sense the root meaning and the Aristotelian tradition are preserved. The new and, in a way, active element in the Christian conception is that spontaneity and the creative power of love are kindled by *passio* (fundamentally, this too is Aristotelian). But *passion* always comes from the superhuman powers above or below and is received and suffered as a glorious or terrible gift." Erich Auerbach, "Excursus: *Gloria Passionis*," in *Literary Language and Its Public in Late Latin Antiquity and the Middle Ages*, trans. Ralph Manheim (New York: Bollinger Foundation, 1965), 67–81. This Christian condemnation of apathy still can be found in places such as the Web site Noapathy.org, which foregrounds this rather odd passage from Revelation 3.15–16: "I know your works, that you are neither cold nor hot. I would that you were cold or hot. So, because you are LUKEWARM, and neither cold nor hot, I am about to vomit you out of My mouth" (www.noapathy.org, accessed April 24, 2005). In this case, apathy is considered morally repugnant because it extends to the sacred, where some sort of passion is more appropriate; in its neutrality, apathy is deeply suspect.

15. Daniel M. Gross, "Melanchthon's Rhetoric and the Practical Origins of Reformation Human Science," *History of the Human Sciences* 13, no. 3 (2000): 5–22.

were natural necessities that mediated the supernatural, whether divine, artistic, or political. Rather than squelching the passions on the advice of Seneca, one could put passions to use on the advice of Aristotle—or more specifically, on the advice one could find in the *De anima*, the *Nicomachean Ethics*, and in the second book of Aristotle's *Rhetoric*.

Only a deficient soul can be moved at all. In Aristotle's *De anima*, this claim is put in terms of basic physics: "for movement is . . . an activity of what is imperfect, activity in the unqualified sense, i.e. that of what has been perfected, is different from movement" (*De anima*, 431a6–9). So where Pufendorf's static political science would seem to work backward from this end point of physical perfection, we would expect political art in the Aristotelian tradition to treat the dynamics of *im*perfection. In a passage from the *Politics* consequential for the post-Westphalian era of relative peace on the European continent, Aristotle appears to defend three "perfect" sorts of government—monarchy, aristocracy, and constitutional government—against three corresponding forms of perversion: tyranny, oligarchy, and democracy (*Politics*, 1279a28–32). Indeed, Aristotle frequently works with this simplified scheme of the "natural" and the "perverse" to highlight the various types of self-interest that cripple a commonwealth. But upon closer scrutiny it becomes apparent how Aristotle does finally accommodate his politics to an ontology of privation, where nature, or *physis*, is defined as "a principle of motion and change" (*Physics*, 200b12). Writing about ostensibly natural aristocratic and constitutional forms of government, Aristotle admits, "the truth is, that they all fall short of the most perfect form of government, and so they are reckoned among perversions, and the really perverted forms are perversions of these" (*Politics*, 1293b25–27). The most perfect form of government— and thus the only one that would be truly "natural"—would be one in which a philosopher king of unassailable virtue dictated public interest from a position outside the law. Aristotle concedes, however, that "passion perverts the minds of rulers, even when they are the best of men" (*Politics*, 1287a31). Therefore, in the practical world, politics will be more a matter of mastering emotional habits of the incorrigible than of polishing the naturally pristine; more a question of practical dynamics than of philosophical necessity.

Politics is about moving people. It is in certain respects a science, according to Aristotle, in others a matter of practical wisdom. But as early modern political theorists would reiterate, politics is also a matter of art.[16] For politics is not just about things necessary and eternal, nor is it just a matter of good judgment in a given situation. It is also about seeing in concrete terms how things might be otherwise and doing something about it. The politician, in other words, is specially skilled in the rhetorical art of seeing how vivid possibilities might be painted in the imagination. For instance, Cydias invoked a productive kind of shame, according to Aristotle, by asking those engaged in a suspect debate about land allotment to imagine the scrutiny of all the Greeks (1384b32–35). In Aristotle's *Nicomachean Ethics*, we learn that art is generally "concerned with coming into being and contriving and seeing how something may come to be among things that are capable of being and not being." In fact, there is no art of things that exist by necessity, nor of things that exist "by nature," for such things have their first principles in themselves (think of a mathematician looking for objective principles of geometry).[17] Rhetoric is a sort of theoretical art that contrives human affairs, or once again in Aristotle's famous formulation, it is the "ability in each case to see the available means of persuasion" (*dynamis peri hekaston theoresai endekhomenon pithanon*).[18] And since the proper domain of politics is the contingent—its substance the weaknesses of people, their passions, proclivities, and dreams—it should be no surprise that rhetoric serves as politics' first auxiliary art.

16. "Now laws are as it were the 'works' of the political art." Aristotle, *Nicomachean Ethics*, 1181a22.

17. Aristotle, *Nicomachean Ethics*, 1140a11–15. This translation of Aristotle's definition of art comes from Aristotle, *On Rhetoric*, appendix 1B (see introduction, n. 1).

18. Aristotle, *On Rhetoric*, 1355b26.

That natural-law theorists in the tradition of Grotius drew heavily upon a Stoic theory of the passions is a scholarly commonplace. Less well known is the profound impact of Aristotle's rhetorical and ethical theory of the passions on seventeenth-century political thought and beyond.[19] Here, briefly, is how Aristotle's *Ethics* plausibly outlined the mechanics that train passions of the irrational soul to moral virtue—a crucial step in his argument against apathy as a basic moral principle. Aristotle begins by breaking down the soul into rational and irrational elements that correspond, on the one hand, to categories of philosophical and practical wisdom and, on the other, to intellectual and moral virtue. The irrational element of the soul is then further divided into a vegetative element and an appetitive, or desiring, element. And since it can be "in some sense persuaded by a rational principle," it is this desiring element that Aristotle claims is the proper object of a moral science. (Evidence for this, according to Aristotle, can be induced from the observable fact that people function rhetorically: that is, they advise, reprove, exhort, and so on; 1102b35–1103a1). Here we find the key to Aristotelian ethics so important for early modern human science: moral virtue is by definition *un*natural because it is subject to training in a rhetorical mode. Or in positive terms, moral virtue is a matter of habit—a second nature posing as first (1152a30–34).

> Virtue being of two kinds, intellectual and moral, intellectual virtue in the main owes both its birth and its growth to teaching (for which reason it requires experience and time), while moral virtue comes about as a result of habit, whence also its name *ethike* is one that is

19. See chapter 1. This neglect is due in part to Dilthey, who misleadingly assimilates Aristotle to the position of a metaphysical dualist at odds with the modern anthropology. See Dilthey, "Die Funktion der Anthropologie," 435 (see chap. 2, n. 11). Aristotle's argument *against* mind/body dualism appears in *De anima*, 407b13–25 and 412a–412b. For a more measured treatment of Aristotle's theory of the soul in the seventeenth century, see Walter Pagel, *From Paracelsus to Van Helmont: Studies in Renaissance Medicine and Science*, ed. Marianne Winder (London: Variorum Reprints, 1986), esp. "Helmont, Leibniz, Stahl," "Aristotle and Seventeenth-Century Biological Thought," and "Harvey and Glisson on Irritability."

formed by a slight variation from the word *ethos* (habit). From this it is also plain that *none of the moral virtues arises in us by nature*; for nothing that exists by nature can form a habit contrary to its nature. For instance the stone which by nature moves downwards cannot be habituated to move upwards, not even if one tries to train it by throwing it up ten thousand times; nor can fire be habituated to move downwards, nor can anything else that by nature behaves in one way be trained to behave in another. Neither by nature, then, nor contrary to nature do the virtues arise in us; rather we are adapted by nature to receive them, and are made perfect by habit. (1103b14–25; my italics)

So the role of the human scientist—whether in the person of an artist, teacher, or politician—is to bypass those natural dispositions that are untrainable (we cannot, for instance, teach a child to fly instead of walk) and work instead on our capacity for the unnatural: for instance, the capacity to build a building, play a lyre, or act in the common interest (1102b30–1103b2). "Both art and virtue are always concerned with what is harder" (1105a9–10), Aristotle astutely remarks, and in the political realm the hardest thing is to come up with a constitution that gives nature of this second kind a secure, institutional form. "This is confirmed by what happens in states," Aristotle continues, "for legislators make the citizens good by forming habits in them, and this is the wish of every legislator, and those who do not effect it miss the mark, and it is in this that a good constitution differs from a bad one" (1103b3–6).

A good constitution, then, is the institutional form of good habits. But rather than simply contrasting good civic habits to antisocial outbursts, Aristotle has a more interesting story to tell about the political utility of the passions. In contrast to the Academic philosopher Speusippus, who defines virtue as "certain states of impassivity and rest" (1104b19–30), Aristotle insists that virtue is concerned with public actions and public passions in the most intimate manner. Virtues, Aristotle clarifies, are the result of actions and passions appropriately tailored to circumstance: "For instance, both fear and confidence and appetite and anger and pity and in general pleasure and pain may be felt both too much and too little, and in both cases not well; but to feel them at the right times, with reference to the right objects, towards the right people, with the right motive, and in the right way, is what is both intermediate and best, and this is characteristic of virtue" (1106b17–24). Though it is a "rhetorical," or context-sensitive, theory of virtue at odds with Stoic rigor, this famous Peripatetic doctrine of the mean nevertheless seems a poor fit with the more enthusiastic Christian position that would find its clearest articulation in Augustine and the early church fathers. Certain virtues, such as the love of God, cannot be overdone, whereas certain passions, such as spite or jealousy, admit no virtuous intermediate (*metriopatheia*). However, this type of qualification never escaped Aristotle. In fact, he states bluntly "not every action nor every passion admits of a mean; for some have names that already imply badness, e.g., spite, shamelessness, envy, and in the case of actions adultery, theft, murder; for all of these and suchlike things imply by their names that they are themselves bad, and not the excesses or deficiencies of them." (There is, for instance, no such thing as committing adultery with the right woman, at the right time, and in the right way; 1107a9–17).

As a result of this semantic qualification, Aristotle's ethical theory of the passions is in the end adaptable to early modern concerns both religious and political. For political theorists on the Continent and in England, the goal was to articulate an institutional forum that trained unruly passions to virtuous habits but at the same time left room for even the most extreme Christian sentiments. And these theorists could turn to Aristotle's *Politics* for assistance in thinking through which of the state constitutions best performed this unnatural function in a manner compatible with Christianity. In combining rich and poor in one political body, Aristotle suggests, a democratic constitution provides a forum for achieving honor independent of jealousy and greed—those ignoble passions oriented toward wealth. By contrast, tyranny is unstable because it induces unpredictable passions of hatred and contempt in its citizens.[20] Picking up Aristotle's mode of political analysis, Hobbes will then explain, for instance, that religion is a continuation of affective politics by other means: considering the afterlife multiplies the fear of punishment and the pleasure in reward that regulate behavior in earthly life. Meanwhile, Aristotle's *Rhetoric* could assist Hobbes and other political theorists as they discussed how mundane institutions such as the law courts and the assembly might best negotiate the affective politics of everyday life.[21]

A Critical History of Apathy: Seneca to Sorabji

This reason versus passion debate becomes interesting when it challenges our late-modern pieties such as the rational choice model in the social sciences (which Hobbes contradicts in his argument that political deliberation operates completely within a sphere of socially constituted fears, hopes, and desires) or when the debate takes concrete historical form (as it does when Scottish Commissioner George Gillespie informs the rebellious House of Commons on March 27, 1644, that political action, paradoxically,

---

20. Aristotle, *Politics*, 2.7, 2.9, 3.15; esp. 1308b28–30; on tyranny, 5.10.

21. See chapter 1. Hobbes was the first to translate Aristotle's *Rhetoric* into English (1638), and early in his career Hobbes considered rhetoric the primary vehicle of civil society. The relationship between human nature and rhetorical art in Hobbes's early work is well expressed in a contemporary preface to his abridged translation of Aristotle: "Mr. Hobbes in his book of *Human Nature* had already described man, with an exactness almost equal to the original draught of nature; and in his *Elements of Law* laid down the constitution of government, and shown by what armed reason it is maintained: and having demonstrated in the state of nature the primitive art of fighting to be the only medium whereby men procured their ends, did in this design to show what power in societies has succeeded to reign in its stead, I mean the art of speaking; which by use of common places of probability, and knowledge in the manners and passions of mankind, through the working of belief is able to bring about whatsoever interest." In *The English Works of Thomas Hobbes of Malmesbury*, vol. 6, ed. Sir William Molesworth (London: Bohn, 1840; reprint, Aalen: Scientia, 1966), 421. Though similar to war, rhetoric is more suited to transforming men's and women's perverse nature, and thus more exact in achieving their supernatural (i.e., civilized) interests. At least in the earlier "humanist" phase of Hobbes's career, rhetoric is antidote to perverse human nature par excellence.

is open only to those who are ashamed, confounded, and humbled; see chapters 1 and 3, respectively). Reduced to platitudes of the sort compiled above by Christoph Lehmann and circulated as rhetorical commonplaces to this day, however, the debate between reason and passion is fairly lifeless. Equally uninspiring is a cyclical model of intellectual history that casts reason and passion as opposite poles in a perennial debate that runs through the ancient disciplines of philosophy and rhetoric or through periods of Enlightenment and romanticism, then on through our day. In what follows, I read critically Seneca's *On Anger* to show what is missed in the simple model of intellectual history: namely, the constitutive power of emotion—and its absence—that configures a social field in its historical specificity.

Here is the key passage from book 3 of Seneca's *On Anger*, in the section on moral therapy called " How to Avoid the Onset of Anger":

> We may find help in that sound advice of Democritus which points to tranquility "if we refrain from doing many things, either in private or in public, or anything beyond our powers." If one runs off on many different activities, one will never have the luck to spend a day without some annoyance arising, from someone or something, to dispose the mind to anger. If one hurries through the crowded parts of the city, one cannot help knocking into many people; one is bound to slip, to be held back, to be splashed. In the same way, if one's course of life is fragmented and always taking a different direction, many things will get in the way and there will be much to complain about—one man has disappointed us, another put us off, a third cut us short; our plans did not take the course that we intended. No one has fortune so much on his side as always to answer to his wishes, if he attempts many things. As a result, should he do so, he finds his plans thwarted and becomes impatient with people and things. At the slightest provocation he loses his temper with the person involved, with the matter in hand, with his position, with his luck, with himself. So if the mind is to have the possibility of being calm, it must not be tossed about nor, as I said, exhausted by doing many things or anything too ambitious for its powers. (3.6)

First, let me situate this passage in my broader polemic: according to Seneca, anger and its shadow, apathy, are human phenomena that definitively exceed their biology. Analysis that would focus either upon the physical expression of anger or upon the feeling of anger would be profoundly inadequate; diagnosis of a chemical imbalance would be inaccurate, and treatment by way of pharmacology irresponsible.

No doubt the biology of emotion that has such currency in our day can be justified by arguing that only a theory of evolution adequately explains how an emotion like anger or empathy can be shared between human and nonhuman animals.[22] Or, alternatively, a biological treatment of emotion can be justified on narrow therapeutic grounds whereby successful "anger management" includes some direct treatment of physiological pain or physical aggression. What Seneca's analysis shows, however, is that the emotional complex of anger and apathy cannot be exhausted by its description in biological, physiological, or any other natural-scientific terms. In this case, scientific terms would be, in fact, thoroughly inappropriate. Anger and apathy as human phenomena are essentially and irreducibly social, and as such they demand an interpretive social theory (and not a strict social science) that shows a special sensitivity toward what both Aristotle and Seneca consider "unnatural," or cultural, phenomena, such as language, social habit, political differentiation, and historical circumstance. Technically, all these phenomena can themselves be treated exclusively in scientific terms—be it through our science of linguistics, political science, or sociobiology—but not without a dramatic reduction of the phenomenon at hand.

According to Seneca, anger and apathy are directly correlated, first, with one's power in a contoured world of meaningful things and people and, second, with one's attitude toward the constraints and possibilities that world imposes. Moreover, one's power is not some biological coefficient distributed to the organism at birth

22. Stephanie D. Preston and Frans B. M. de Waal, "Empathy: Its Ultimate and Proximate Bases," *Behavioral and Brain Sciences* 25, no. 1 (2002).

and then negotiated in the fight for survival. It is a direct function of one's position in a world where the power of a single person depends upon the cultural capital accrued to one's social position and also upon the expense paid in deference by those cast as inferior. We see Seneca's subject in this example not as a sovereign or a slave, for instance, but rather as a cosmopolitan male of moderate means who apparently has the power to dream of pastoral retreat and deferential treatment but suffers instead the daily insults of having his tunic splashed. And in this case, interestingly, an emotion such as anger functions in an economy of scarcity where a moral premium is placed on scarcity itself. For apathy (or "tranquility" in this passage) signifies under Seneca's description neither the absence of power nor social irresponsibility. Instead, it signifies for Seneca peace with one's place in the world: that is to say, a realistic and fully engaged assessment of how one's power is differentially constituted and exercised. The perfectly tranquil person desires nothing more than his or her social position affords, and he or she studiously avoids any situation in which that social position might be threatened—for instance, in the busy streets of Rome, where a man of moderate means inadvertently might be treated with disrespect. He picks companions who are "submissive, polite and gracious," though not to the point of obsequiousness (3.8.5), dodges heavier intellectual activities (3.9.1), and even avoids the forum or the law courts if he is particularly disposed to anger (3.9.3).

Where Seneca remarks that even the weakest are often angry with the most powerful, even though the weak have no power to punish (1.2.2), someone like Paul Ekman might detect a theory of universal emotion in which the same basic emotions are shared equally and to the same degree across different cultures and different sorts of people—some displaying emotions openly, where others suppress them. But if we fixate upon this apparent universalism, we distort Seneca's theory of emotion dramatically.[23]

23. Seneca, *On Favors*, 3.28.1. In *Emotion and Peace of Mind* (see introduction, n. 3) and elsewhere, Richard Sorabji in fact champions the universal humanism of the

In building his general argument that emotions are voluntary, Seneca does provide evidence that anger can be eradicated from the lives of monarchs and subordinates alike. But there the emotional similarity between these two sorts of people ends. Simply put, the higher one's social status, the more frequently one is subject to the offensive behavior of others and, therefore, the more often one can become angry. Remember, for Seneca getting one's toes stepped on or overtures ignored does not necessarily provoke anger (or its inverse, studied detachment). However, getting one's toes stepped on or overtures ignored *undeservedly* does. Since, socially speaking, the slave deserves little compared to the monarch, his capacity for anger also differs dramatically. Indeed, it would be wildly misleading to organize my analysis around the trivial observation that both have the capacity for anger. In Seneca's subtle analysis, anger and apathy are instead treated as scarce resources.

Here is an example that shows concretely how emotion and its absence configure a particular set of relationships between people. Having declared war upon the Scythians encircling his eastern border, Darius I, the third Achaemenid king of Persia, was asked by Oeobazus, an elderly noble with three sons, to let one stay behind to console his father, while employing the services of the other two. Promising to go beyond what was asked and excuse all three, Darius then killed the sons in front of their

---

Stoics. Although the Stoic doctrine of indifference seems incompatible with fellow-feeling, "fellow-feeling," asserts Sorabji, is in fact "a centerpiece of Stoic moral theory. For the Stoics argue that it is in accordance with nature and is right to treat all human beings, even slaves, as belonging, metaphorically speaking, in the same household (*oikos*), because all humans are rational" (174). My argument is that although this universal humanism can be found in Stoic philosophy as it can be found in the U.S. Constitution and other Enlightenment documents, it isn't a centerpiece. That is to say, what's characteristic and interesting about Stoic philosophy—what seems to be worth spilled ink and writerly fireworks—isn't this universal claim but rather the subtle analysis of practical situations of the sort treated by Seneca above, where technologies of social differentiation and moral development are at issue. When we emphasize the universal humanism of the Stoics in the manner of Sorabji and Martha Nussbaum, we bring our own liberal sensibilities to bear.

father because, he explained, it would have been cruel to take them all (3.16.3). According to Seneca, this example is illuminating because it shows how Darius, like most potentates through Alexander and Caligula, treated anger as "a badge of royalty." Of course this is a prerogative of power not afforded everybody, as Seneca clarifies in a related observation: most tyrants who fail to control their emotions fall victim to individual assassins or to whole groups "whom a common distress has forced to *pool their anger*" (3.16.2; my italics). Apparently, for an absolute monarch (as opposed to an elected president, for instance), anger lies potentially in the relationship to every subject, in every word and every act, no matter how insignificant. As the case of Darius demonstrates, however, a monarch's fathomless capacity for anger is not contained within the borders of the individual, nor is it housed in the monarch's nature equally and to the same degree as the anger of his or her subjects, who in comparison lack only the adequate means of expression. The monarch's anger has a significantly *disproportionate* effect on the emotional economy writ large. Its capacity to become reified in the institutions and practices of government—from the dictates of law to the body of the executioner—determines disproportionately the emotional economy of the monarch's political subjects and greatly exceeds the capacity for anger afforded the subjects themselves. Likewise, the monarch's capacity for apathy dramatically exceeds that of his or her subjects, and therefore, in this regard, the monarch's influence on the emotional economy is again disproportionate. Thus, in his treatise *On Mercy*, composed for the young emperor Nero, Seneca advises prophylactically that "the gentleness of your mind will be transmitted to others; little by little, it will be diffused over the whole body of the empire."[24] A lot of good that did.

In Seneca's model, to summarize, the scope of anger afforded monarchs, aristocrats, soldiers, noncitizens of Rome, women, children, and slaves varies dramatically, and, structurally speaking, the anger afforded one will come at the expense of another.

24. Seneca, *On Mercy*, 2.2.1.

The scope of apathy functions in the analogous manner, as a kind of shadow that promises to replace the frustrating excess of social ambition (i.e., anger) with the resignation that comes with accepting one's place in the world. Apathy, in other words, is a shadow phenomenon that refers at each point to the emotional economy writ large. And we should note that Seneca was not the only Stoically minded Latin author who considered emotion in an economy of scarcity. For instance, in his *Tusculan Disputations* treatment of emotional disturbances that actually become sicknesses of character, Cicero, the technically Academic philosopher, provides the telling example of *mulierositas* (Greek *philogunia*), or "liking for women," which is akin to other sicknesses such as gluttony (*liguritio*) and fondness for wine (*vinulentia*) but different from the aversion called "hatred of women," or *mulierum odium* (Greek *misogunia*).[25] The fact that there is no analogous terminology for liking or hating men reveals how emotional economies function unevenly for Cicero as well, institutionalizing in language and social practice a particular set of relationships.

The next question is what happened in early modernity to this sophisticated, social analysis of emotion and its absence, eventually diminishing it to the biology of emotion and psychological individualism dominant today, even in the work of our most respected humanists. Comparing Hobbes and Henry More on apathy will help establish the answer.

The Demise of Apathy as a Public Virtue

My analysis of Seneca's Stoicism shows how little difference it can make in the end whether emotions are considered good or bad. For even those who would uniformly wish them away realize that emotions are an important facet of the practical world—fallen, unnatural, and flawed as it is. In fact, the work of Seneca and

25. Cicero, *Tusculan Disputations*, 4.2.25. See also Margaret Graver, *Cicero on the Emotions: Tusculan Disputations 3 and 4* (Chicago: University of Chicago Press, 2002), 150.

other Stoic philosophers demonstrates that some of the most sophisticated discussions of emotion actually come in works devoted to their extirpation, a fact not lost on our most respected commentators on classical philosophies of emotion, including Richard Sorabji and Martha Nussbaum. What matters, generally speaking, is less the attitude toward emotion than the analysis; and what matters more specifically for my purposes is the analysis that explicitly links psyche and politics, allowing us to see how emotions and their absence exceed biology and help shape the public sphere. In this special regard, Seneca does a very good job indeed, Sorabji and Nussbaum less so.

In *Emotion and Peace of Mind: From Stoic Agitation to Christian Temptation*, Richard Sorabji renders Stoicism palatable by making sense of implausible elements, such as the claim that emotions are completely voluntary (45), and purging Stoicism of its most objectionable elements, such as the radical doctrine of indifference (169). Key to Sorabji's argumentative strategy, and especially his defense of Seneca (66ff.), is a distinction typically overlooked by critics of Stoicism between "first movements" (*primus motus*, or *propatheiai* in Greek), such as startling, tears, and sexual arousal,[26] and emotions in a strict sense that consist in judgments: specifically, the judgment that something at hand is good or bad and the judgment that a particular reaction is appropriate (2–6). This strategy of distinction is justified by Sorabji in scientific terms by citing the brain science of Antonio Damasio and especially Joseph LeDoux, who (as I have described) distinguishes between an amygdala reaction, such as startling at a snake, and a reaction of the cerebral cortex that allows us to respond appropriately in the manner we characterize as "fear" (144–55). According to Sorabji, LeDoux's amygdala reactions correspond roughly to Stoic first movements, and cerebral cortex reactions to Stoic emotion-as-judgment. Sorabji's interpretive claim is that Stoics from Chrysippus and Posidonius to Seneca and Origen acknowledged the ineradicable nature of first movements but

26. Graver, *Cicero on the Emotions*, 126.

believed that, with the right kind of cognitive therapy, one could eradicate the negative emotions that follow, such as grief, anger, and fear. On Sorabji's view then, "counterproductive emotions" manifest in everyday experiences such as road rage or the anxieties of office politics can be treated in Stoic fashion not by gritting your teeth but by "seeing things differently, so that you do not need to grit your teeth" (1–2).

This approach may work. Perhaps, like the Roman knight Pastor, who responded to Caligula's brutal killing of one son with the calming thought that he had another (*On Anger* 2.33), we can respond to one unfairly denied job opportunity with the calming thought that we may get another. Or, as Paul Ekman might recommend, we can put on a smile in order to make us more relaxed[27] or de-stress on the treadmill (i.e., noncognitive therapies). But with these solutions, the richness of Seneca's social analysis of emotion is flattened. What we are left with is a harmless form of self-help psychology justified in terms of the latest brain science but not in terms of a sophisticated social theory that we would expect from a humanist and professor of rhetoric such as Sorabji. *Emotion and Peace of Mind* is an outstanding book when it comes both to distinguishing between the range of Stoic philosophies of emotion and to demonstrating how a limited version of Stoicism might be saved from its detractors in late antiquity and beyond. It is less good when it comes to saving Stoic social analysis from the distortions of modern individualism and scientism. In fact, Sorabji claims that one of the limitations on Stoic cognitive therapy is that, unlike the "up-to-date" account of pop psychologist Daniel Goleman (!), Stoics concentrate their attention on understanding one's own emotions, "not the emotional effect of one person on another, nor the emotions of others, except insofar as these bear directly on how to control one's own" (153). The example of this exception Sorabji draws from *On Anger*, 2.28, where Seneca suggests that you may control your own anger by reflecting: "I, too, have before now committed the offense I am

---

27. Sorabji, *Emotion and Peace of Mind*, 151 (see introduction, n. 3).

complaining of." Hopefully, I have shown how Seneca's social analysis of emotion goes much further.

Mildly put, "missed opportunity" can also characterize my criticism of Martha Nussbaum. And again I think that the prestige of scientific explanations does something to temper the resourcefulness of this skilled humanist, at least insofar as she grounds her theory of compassion in *Upheavals of Thought: The Intelligence of Emotions*. Like Sorabji, Nussbaum claims (incorrectly, I believe) that the original Stoics "said nothing about how variations in [social] norms entail variations in emotion," but, unlike Sorabji, Nussbaum takes this apparent shortcoming as a positive challenge: one important modification Nussbaum sets out to make in the Stoic theory of emotion is to offer an account of the role "social construction" plays in emotional life (6). And in this regard Nussbaum does make strong claims that go well beyond Sorabji: "in an ethical and social/political creature, emotions themselves are ethical and social/political, parts of an answer to the questions, 'What is worth caring about?' 'How should I live?'" (149). By way of example, Nussbaum explains that norms manifest in literature can help constitute what is considered "an appropriate object of sympathy" (167), while the oppression sometimes manifest in religion and other cultural institutions can help constitute the self-hatred that wrongly justifies suffering (309). So according to Nussbaum, the cognitive element of emotion is indeed highly malleable, and therefore it is also disproportionately subject to manipulation by the rhetoric of "sympathy entrepreneurs" such as politicians and journalists. Some, like sympathy entrepreneur Franklin Delano Roosevelt, therefore make a "considerable difference to public emotion" because they have ready access to the means of communication, while others presumably make less of an impact because of their modest social position. Clearly Nussbaum does understand how emotional life varies from person to person in what I have been calling an "emotional economy," and at times she demonstrates skill in tying this variation not just to individual temperament but to culture and history. However, Nussbaum goes terribly wrong, in my opinion, when she finally embeds her critical observations in normative and scientific terms. A central challenge Nussbaum sets herself in *Upheavals of Thought* is to go beyond the pessimistic social theory that simply analyzes the relationship between power and the scope of compassion, providing instead a normative theory along the lines of Adam Smith that would show on what ground the circle of compassion might be expanded universally (66, 341n, 345). Not surprisingly, this effort also founders on the same ground as Smith.

"Let us stipulate," Nussbaum ventures in the prescriptive portion of her book, "that a reasonable set of judgments . . . for the public culture of a pluralistic liberal democracy, would involve an extension of something like equal respect and concern to all citizens of whatever race, sex, class, or ethnic origin" (420–21). But on what ground does Nussbaum justify this starting point, and how does she explain the consequent reasonableness of expanding compassion along particular lines? Though admittedly the rules of formal argumentation allow a stipulative starting point without justification, our common sense looks for some justification anyway, even if that requires attention to informal arguments and mere inferences. Widening the circle of concern on normative grounds ultimately makes sense to Nussbaum, it would seem, because doing so would coincide with a theory of evolution. In a key passage, Nussbaum explains that the reason why compassion typically leads to helping behaviors rather than to sadistic torturing is that we have "psychological mechanisms that tend in that direction" rather than the opposite—a conclusion Nussbaum reaches on the evidence provided by primatologist Frans de Waal and evolutionary biologists Elliott Sober and David Sloan Wilson (338). There is, in other words, an evolutionary advantage to altruistic behavior in terms of a theory of group selection, whereas "normatively problematic" emotions such as envy, shame, and disgust are presumably disadvantageous (300, 342–50). Splendid! I think. If we stick around this planet long enough, maybe our normatively problematic emotions will atrophy, like our tailbones. Likewise, in a section on "nonreductionistic" physiological accounts of emotion that foregrounds the work

of Joseph LeDoux and Antonio Damasio, Nussbaum acknowledges practical limitations on the brain science of emotion, such as
the ethical problem of performing vivisections, but waxes hopeful
that neuroscience might one day produce a kind of uniformity
and constancy across cases, giving us "reason to incorporate a
concrete description of a specific type of neurological function-
ing into the definition of a particular emotion type" (119). If
she is truly so inclined, Nussbaum will certainly find satisfactory
neurological descriptions that help her define particular emotions, just as Aristotle once defined anger in *De anima* as a
boiling of the blood or warm substance around the heart. The
problem is not that Nussbaum completely reduces emotion to
its neurological function, but rather that she allows this material
consideration to overwhelm what Aristotle called the competing
"dialectical" consideration, where anger might be defined as the
appetite for returning pain (*De anima*, 403a26–b9). *De rigueur*
in Anglo-American philosophical circles, Nussbaum's lurking
question, Is my theory of emotion compatible with the latest
and most compelling scientific evidence? subtly distorts what she
sees and how she sees it.

   In short, what happens when Nussbaum casually situates her
critical social analysis of emotion with respect to these normative
and scientific considerations is that she is then tempted to classify complex emotions according to their evolutionary function as
"advantageous" or "disadvantageous," losing thereby her capacity
to map with any degree of sensitivity the culturally specific in-
terconnections of psyche and politics evident in the work of
Seneca and others. Instead, we get lists of "The Central Human
Capabilities" that *every* society ought to guarantee its citizens
(416) and creepy (as well as self-serving) Smithian descriptions of
what the "ideal" spectator looks like when she judges how human
flourishing can be maximized. "Equipped with her general conception of human flourishing," Nussbaum imagines,

> the spectator looks at a world in which people suffer hunger, disabil-
> ity, disease, slavery, through no fault of their own. She believes that

goods such as food, health, citizenship, freedom, do matter. And yet she acknowledges, as well, that it is uncertain whether she herself will remain among the safe and privileged ones to whom such goods are stably guaranteed. She acknowledges that the lot of the beggar might be (or become) her own. This leads her to turn her thoughts outward, asking about society's general arrangement for the allocation of goods and resources. Given the uncertainty of life, she will be inclined, other things being equal, to want a society in which the lot of the worst off—of the poor, of people defeated in war, of women, of servants—is as good as it can be. Self-interest itself, via thought about shared vulnerabilities, promotes the selection of principles that raise society's floor. (321)

Noble sentiments indeed; but there is a problem. The only sort of character who would seem to approximate this ideal is someone who knows that she is *not* the oppressed or even the average sort of person subject to bad judgment "skewed by inattention, or bad social teaching, or by some false theory of human life" (310). Rather, she is presumably someone whose attention is fixed, who has enjoyed the best social teaching, and who (therefore?) has a correct theory of human life. Who else, after all, but Nussbaum herself?

In the end, Nussbaum's universal ambitions do run up against the Scylla and Charybdis of biological reduction and the problem of the participant observer. As opposed to an embedded scientific theory, a theory of human life cannot be considered "correct" or "incorrect" from anywhere except from a God's-eye perspective, and when a mere mortal makes the effort to apply any particular theory of human life universally, the prejudices of that theorist (or observer) are typically built into the project without proper justification and applied to other people without adequate sensitivity. "Ethical imperialism" is, of course, a standard postcolonial critique of the liberal perspective on universal human nature and universal human rights, and it is a critique Nussbaum grapples with in part by arguing for the possibility of some perspectives suffering fewer distortions than others,[28] and in part by aligning

28. Here is one of Nussbaum's key examples: "R, a woman in a rural village in India, is severely undernourished, and unable to get more than a first-grade education. She

herself with the Stoic ideal of "equal humanity" that she sees as fundamental to Enlightenment political thought (371, also 357, 429). In the end, Nussbaum's project should be favorably distinguished from that of John Rawls and other post-Enlightenment projects insofar as it toys with a critical perspective before retreating to unreflective universalism. But Nussbaum misses the opportunity to justify her critical perspective in more appropriate humanistic terms and thereby reverses any gains she has made in her effort to think ethically about emotion and its absence.

Now remember the initial question of this chapter: How can we analyze apathy as a political problematic, and not just an existential deficiency? It turns out that the theory most helpful in answering this question comes not from the tradition of classical humanism, represented by people like Sorabji and Nussbaum, but rather from a political strain of psychoanalytic theory, represented by Judith Butler in *The Psychic Life of Power: Theories in Subjection*.[29] Instead of contrasting psychic phenomena that are internal, personal, and physiological to political phenomena that are external, impersonal, and social, Butler asks us to consider how particular processes of internalization fabricate "the distinction between interior and exterior life" (19). Reinvesting a Foucauldian analysis of power with psychoanalytic questions about how we come to desire our own oppression, Butler interrogates the mechanisms of law and language that regulate our passionate attachments: for instance, the U.S. military policy of "don't ask, don't tell" that concentrates homosexual identity precisely in its renunciation (82), or the Names Project Quilt that

---

does not think her lot a bad one, since she has no idea what it is to feel healthy, and no idea of the benefits and pleasures of education. So thoroughly has she internalized her culture's views of what is right for women that she believes that she is living a good and flourishing life, as a woman ought to live one." In this case Nussbaum argues that compassion "takes up the onlooker's point of view, making the best judgment the onlooker can make about what is really happening to the person, even when that may differ from the judgment of the person herself." *Upheavals of Thought*, 309 (see chap. 1, n. 8).

29. Judith Butler, *The Psychic Life of Power: Theories in Subjection* (Stanford, CA: Stanford University Press, 1997).

helps shift the psychic topography of gay melancholia toward a public form of grieving and anger (148). Though postmodern by reputation, Butler's project, I would argue, takes up the *early* modern perspective on emotion and its absence that I have shown explicitly characterized by Hobbes and will show later (more or less buried) in the work of David Hume, Sarah Fielding, Adam Smith, and William Perfect, as well as many others working more in the mode of Aristotle's *Rhetoric* than Cartesian natural philosophy. Making explicit these intellectual historical links will illuminate Butler's theory and our early modern literature alike insofar as it helps us rediscover how apathy helps constitute public life.

How again does Hobbes fabricate the distinction between interior and exterior life? As described in chapter 1, he does it by way of a corrective political science whereby the most intimate details of human nature are subject not merely to description but also to intervention. For Hobbes, we are political animals down to the very sinews of our brain, which means that even brain material suffers from systematic distortions that are of social origin. Therefore, it is also subject to a corrective and enhancing political science that would artificially transform brain material in the same manner that optical instruments correct and enhance vision. Moreover, the analysis of a resolutely anti-Stoic thinker such as Hobbes can recall both Aristotle's and Seneca's social analysis of emotion closely insofar as his analysis situates (what are for us) personal or private emotions in a complex political economy where positive emotions are always fabricated at a social cost accounted for in terms of apathy. Take for instance the following discussion from the *Leviathan*, where Hobbes explains which social passions most profoundly affect intellectual difference, or difference in "wit."

It would be a mistake, Hobbes argues, to presume that intellectual differences between people simply proceed from a variable "temper of the brain," because if that were the case then people would differ as much in their sight, hearing, and other senses as they do in their "Fancies, and Discretions." Differences in wit proceed, therefore, from differences in passion, according to Hobbes, "which are different, not onely from the difference of mens complexions; but also from their difference of customes, and education." Which passions, we might then wonder, most affect differences in wit? "The Passions that most of all cause the differences of Wit," Hobbes continues in a Senecan vein, "are principally, the more or lesse Desire of Power, of Riches, of Knowledge, and of Honour. All which may be reduced to the first, that is Desire of Power. For Riches, Knowledge and Honour are but severall sorts of Power." Unlike Seneca, however, Hobbes does not view this desire as a bad thing inherently, since it is precisely the desire for power that stimulates imagination and provides the motivation to make prudent decisions in the real world. "And therefore," Hobbes famously concludes in his diatribe against what he calls "indifference," "a man who has no great Passion for any of these things [i.e., riches, knowledge, and honor]; but is as men terme it indifferent; though he may be so farre a good man, as to be free from giving offence; yet he cannot possibly have either a great Fancy, or much Judgment. For the Thoughts, are to the Desires, as Scouts, and Spies, to range abroad, and find the way to the things Desired" (53).

According to Hobbes, the very substance of our body is determined by the passions of our soul. But unlike either a Cartesian natural philosopher, who would reduce the soul to its mechanical function, or a theologian such as John Preston, who would be interested in the soul as a receptacle for God's love, Hobbes treats the soul by way of an interpretive political science where passions are a function of power. And not just power in some generic or universal sense. As he demonstrates in his subtle analysis of vainglory, the passion that catalyzed the English Civil War, power for Hobbes is historically specific in its formation and differential in its structure. Passions for Hobbes (like Seneca) are a direct function of one's social position: glory is the accurate reflection of one's power and ability in the imagination (42); vainglory, the distortion of one's power and ability provoked primarily by flattery. Hence, vainglory is also the cause of quarrels and ultimately war because it makes men invade "for trifles, as a word, a smile, a different opinion, and any other signe of undervalue, either direct in their Persons, or by reflection in their Kindred, their Friends, their Nation, their Profession, or their Name" (88). Like Seneca's Roman pedestrian subject to the undeserved slights of a careless passerby, Hobbes's Presbyterian is subject to the misevaluation that extends beyond his person to his name and even to his nation as it is constituted in his imagination. Passion, in other words, is a function of social scope, while passion's excess is a function of overheated language, overheated imagination, and other inevitable frictions of a dynamic social system in which the power of one usually comes at the expense of another. Apathy is, by contrast, the inverse of enthusiasm, when one's social value is systematically underestimated, with equally devastating consequences for the smooth operation of civil society.

With Hobbes, the interanimation of psyche and politics thus finds its overt expression precisely at the moment when political science became a viable mode of inquiry justifiable on grounds other than religious, but just before "science" loses its classical association with humanistic knowing and settles definitively into its modern form. In the chapters that follow, I will argue that the interanimation of psyche and politics so evident to Hobbes remains a key issue in the work of David Hume, Sarah Fielding, Adam Smith, William Perfect, and many others through our day who write about emotion, although the explicit analytic framework that would tie psyche to politics becomes increasingly difficult to deploy as it gets buried in the niceties of scientific universalism (awaiting there our deconstruction). In order to get a concrete sense for this increasingly viable alternative to Hobbes, it will be helpful to conclude this chapter by contrasting Hobbes on apathy with one of his Cambridge antagonists, Henry More. More set the pattern for attacks on religious Dissenters for the next one hundred years by associating enthusiasm with unrestrained imagination in his 1656 tract reworked in 1662 under the title "*Enthusiasmus Triumphatus*; or, a Brief Discourse of the Nature,

Causes, Kinds, and Cure of Enthusiasm."[30] It turns out that the difference between Hobbes and More is best revealed in the different ways each configures apathy, revealed, as Butler might say, in the different ways each fabricates the distinction between interior and exterior life. Hobbes considers apathy a dysfunctional social condition, More a functional condition of the psychological individual.

Because for Hobbes the soul itself is a kind of social/political fabric instantiated both in the microcosm of a natural person and in the macrocosm of the "artificial man" as commonwealth (111ff.), it is first and foremost the appropriate object of political science. For More, on the other hand, the soul is a divine deposit subject to natural, mechanical processes, per Descartes, as well as natural and moral corruption, and it is therefore the appropriate object of natural and moral philosophy. Here is More in a revealing passage on the cure of enthusiasm by (1) humility, which More understands as submission to the will of God, (2) reason, which More understands in Cartesian terms as a composure of mind that tests every "high flown & forward Fancy" against common and outward senses, or else a *"clear and distinct Deduction from these,"* and finally (3) by temperance, which he understands to be

> a measurable Abstinence from all hot or heightening meats or drinks, as also from all venereous pleasures and tactuall delights of the Body, from all softness and effeminacy; a constant and peremptory adhesion to the perfectest degree of *Chastity* in the single life, and of *Continency* in wedlock, that can be attain'd to. For it is plain in sundry examples of *Enthusiasm* above named, that the more hidden and lurking fumes of *Lust* had tainted the *Phansies* of those pretenders to *Prophecy* and *Inspiration.*
>
> We will adde also to these, moderate exercise of Body, and reasonable taking of the fresh aire, and due to discrete use of Devotion,

30. Editor's introduction, *"Enthusiasmus Triumphatus;* or, A Brief Discourse of the Nature, Causes, Kinds, and Cure of Enthusiasm," by Henry More, Augustan Reprint Society 118 (Los Angeles: William Andrews Clark Memorial Library, 1966), vi.

whereby the Blood is ventilated and purged from dark oppressing vapors; which a temperate diet, if not fasting, must also accompany: or else the more hot and zealous our addresses are, the more likely they are to bring mischief upon our own heads, they raising the feculency of our intemperance into those more precious parts of the Body, the *Brains* and *Animal Spirits*, and so intoxicating the Mind with fury and wildness. (37–38)

Where imagination for Hobbes is both politically necessary as a means to envision the future (*Leviathan*, 23) and the source of politically dangerous "fancy" (19), for More it is primarily a source of psychological error. For Hobbes excessive and dangerous passions themselves have social causes; for More they are deviations from the psychological norm that are directly caused by material imbalances. Hence, for More, apathy becomes an explicit virtue of the temperate individual but only an implicit civic virtue, whereas for Hobbes, as I have shown, apathy, or "indifference," represents the failure of imagination cultivated by way of social disadvantage.

Where Hobbes (like Butler) analyzes how human institutions of law and language fabricate the distinction between interior and exterior life, More (like Nussbaum) is ultimately interested in the mechanisms of mind that seem to explain human nature. Symptomatically, More's discussion of "political enthusiasm" is contained within a few short examples of famous figures such as David George who suffer from delusions of grandeur (22–26). But despite whatever shortcomings and errors in detail we might now recognize, More's apolitical approach would eventually triumph in the modern disciplines of psychology and in the brain science of emotion. Ultimately, we can learn, however, from our amused reaction to More's claim that excess emotion can be tempered by abstinence from hot and heightening meats and drinks, delights of the body, and any other form of softness or effeminacy, and use this knowledge to sharpen our skepticism about more recent projects that obscure politics by drawing overdetermined connections between biology and emotion. I would suggest, moreover, that we use More's final paradox of the passive mind to exercise our skill in historical deconstruction, without which the emotional politics of modernity remain elusive. According to More, the very triumph of pure reason that is achieved by hardening the mind against fantastic intrusions and seductive pleasures is contingent upon a fundamentally feminized condition of humility in which one totally submits to the will of God. This passions/action, feminine/masculine paradox is the starting point of my next chapter on the virtues of passivity in the English Civil War.

3

Virtues of Passivity
in the English Civil War

My businesse is, merely to persuade you into a *Religious Covenant with God*, as himselfe hath prescribed and commanded; and, his people, in the best times of Reformation, have readily admitted: namely, every man to stirre up himself & to lift up his Soule to take hold of God, to be glued and united to him, in all faithfulnesse, sincerity, care, and diligence, to be onely his for ever.
«CORNELIUS BURGES, *initial fast sermon to the House of Commons, November 17, 1640*»

For the Lawes of Nature (as *Justice*, *Equity*, *Modesty*, *Mercy*, and (in summe) *doing to others, as wee would be done to,*) of themselves, without the terrour of some Power, to cause them to be observed, are contrary to our naturall Passions, that they carry us to Partiality, Pride, Revenge, and the like. And Covenants, without the Sword, are but Words, and of no strength to secure a man at all.
«THOMAS HOBBES, *Leviathan*»

Our late-modern understanding of "reform" presents a paradox. Reform—say, of society, government, or convicts—seems to us the product of activism par excellence, the achievement both of imagination that envisions how a given state of affairs might be otherwise and a strong will able to impose that image upon the world. Martin Luther was a reformer. Oliver Cromwell was a reformer, even a revolutionary. Jeremy Bentham was a reformer.

At the same time, reform quietly suggests to us precisely the opposite: namely, a process undergone, experienced, even suffered. Hannah Arendt put it this way in her famous Aristotelian ruminations on the *Vita Activa*: "Because the actor always moves among and in relation to other acting beings, he is never merely a 'doer' but always and at the same time a sufferer. To do and to suffer are like opposite sides of the same coin."[1] Or in the carefully chosen words of Scottish Commissioner George Gillespie speaking to the rebellious House of Commons March 27, 1644, "acceptable service in the publike Reformation" is open only to those who are ashamed, confounded, and humbled.[2] Reform thus seems to require even of its most potent agents (and not just its patients) precisely the suspension of will that makes room for susceptibility and change, a heightened vulnerability to emotion that comes from somewhere beyond oneself. Indeed, reform in the Puritan context is cleverly described by one scholar of the movement as "a conforming of agencies and acts to *God's* will."[3] In order to see how this paradox shapes both our reading of certain early modern texts and our impoverished, late-modern understanding of public emotion, it is helpful first to consider its succinct formulation: New Left critic Michael Walzer's *The Revolution of the Saints: A Study in the Origins of Radical Politics*. Walzer's 1965 study illustrates symptomatically how a sophisticated, nonreductive, early modern understanding of social passions was incapacitated by a radicalized, late-modern active/passive dyad, which we now tend to read back inappropriately into the early modern context. Complementing the previous two chapters on the dubious triumph of emotional Cartesianism, this chapter continues my genealogical project of reconstituting social emotions by first showing how they have been obscured: in this case obscured by a late-modern fixation on masculine political agency asserted at the expense of

---

1. Hannah Arendt, *The Human Condition* (Chicago: University of Chicago Press, 1958), 190.

2. Quoted in John F. Wilson, *Pulpit in Parliament: Puritanism during the English Civil Wars 1640–1648* (Princeton, NJ: Princeton University Press, 1969), 186–87.

3. Wilson, *Pulpit in Parliament*, 186; my italics.

political "passivism," now relegated to a diminished femininity. And once again in this chapter my analytic strategy is to approach the emotions and their histories not from the dominant perspective of science, but rather from the subordinate perspective of rhetoric.

>>><<<

According to Michael Walzer, medieval society was composed largely of "nonparticipants, inactive men," men of the sort that might appear in the static world of John of Salisbury's *Policraticus.* "Modern" society produced for the first time political "activists" in the strong sense of the word—that is to say, men of conscience capable of political organization, methodical activity in the public sphere, opposition and reform, radical ideology and revolution.[4] For Walzer, much like Jacob Burckhardt and Max Weber before him, "activism" is associated with modern men, while "inactivity" and "passivity" are synonyms that describe premodern men. The goal Walzer then sets himself is to show how "Calvinism taught previously passive men the styles and methods of political activity and enabled them successfully to claim the right of participation in that ongoing system of political action that is the modern state" (18).

Indeed *The Revolution of the Saints* remains to this day both a monument for certain historians of the English Civil War and a key text for understanding a post-1960s version of political activism—activism that has much to admire under any description. I should make it clear that the object of criticism in the analysis that follows is not the achievements and ideals of New Left political activism per se, but rather the rhetoric of activism that foreclosed important political problems that we could broadly designate "emotional." As Hannah Pitkin remarked in her book

4. Michael Walzer, *The Revolution of the Saints: A Study in the Origins of Radical Politics* (Cambridge, MA: Harvard University Press, 1965), 1. Nearly forty years later, Walzer still has a hard time reading humility as a passion. See Walzer, *Politics and Passion: Towards a More Egalitarian Liberalism* (New Haven, CT: Yale University Press, 2004), 114.

on gender and politics in the thought of Niccolò Machiavelli, "activism," or more precisely republican activism, has been linked since classical antiquity to manly military glory and to disdain for the household, the private, the personal.[5] And though one might expect political thinkers on the Left to consider this sort of gendered political history, it remains unarticulated in both Hannah Arendt's revival of Athenian political ideals and in the sort of New Left politics formulated by Michael Walzer.

Walzer overwrites the rich early modern language of political passivity with a relatively flat late-modern language of political activity, thereby producing a rhetoric of reformation shot through with contradictions. It's helpful to look closely at the language in which these contradictions are sustained, because they continue to characterize a meaningful cul-de-sac of our own linguistic and conceptual possibilities. "If we have the honor to be God's instruments," Edward Corbett told the newly assembled House of Commons in 1642, "we must do the office of instruments and be active ... we must go along with Providence" (258). Indeed, Walzer later suggests that this is "one of the most fundamental doctrines of radical politics" first established by the revolutionary saints of the English Civil War: that "men unwilling to be instruments have no right—whatever their social status—to be magistrates" (262). Elsewhere, Walzer identifies covenant theology in equally paradoxical terms as "a new, active and *willing obedience* to command" (167; my italics). Don't these passages present a paradox difficult to resolve in our current language of politics? What on earth is "the office of instruments"? How is one simultaneously a passive instrument of God going along with Providence and politically active in the sense Walzer wants to suggest? These questions are neglected in Walzer's scheme. Walzer's reading of the Corbett passage subordinates the Saint's instrumentality to his political activism; magistrates of the revolutionary parliaments were "instruments" only insofar as they subordinated their

5. Hanna Fenichel Pitkin, *Fortune Is a Woman: Gender and Politics in the Thought of Niccolò Machiavelli* (Berkeley: University of California Press, 1984), 6.

limited (courtly) interests to the greater (protoliberal) interests of a godly commonwealth. In other words, Walzer, like many social critics of his generation, is unable to articulate the rhetoric of passions deeply woven into the language of Corbett and his fellow saints, because he reads the material from the Age of Reason backward.

Humiliation and War

Looking back in *Behemoth* at the tumultuous period of English history between 1640 and 1660, a far from impartial Thomas Hobbes concluded that only the corruption and seduction of the people could explain the utter breakdown of authority and that chief among the seducers were "Minister's (as they call'd themselves) of Christ" (quoted in Wilson, 3).[6] Endowed, according to Hobbes, with a "histrionique faculty," these "Ambitious Ignorant Orators" preached rebellion from the pulpit and deeply influenced the Houses of Parliament, especially the Commons (Wilson, 4). After the 1660 Restoration, Charles II's minister Edward Hyde Earl of Clarendon recognized the extraordinary influence of two such preachers when he objected in *History of the Rebellion* that "the archbishop of Canterbury had never so great an influence upon the counsels at Court as Dr. Burgess and Mr. Marshall had then upon the Houses" (quoted in Trevor-Roper, 298). Hobbes and Clarendon well understood that the battle for the hearts and minds of the English people had been lost long before defeat on the battlefield, and they considered parliamentary rhetoric to blame. This seditious rhetoric had been disseminated in the dynamic print culture that emerged after the Laudian censorship of the 1620s and 1630s, broadcasting to an unprecedented degree a turning of the parliamentary pulpit to

6. The discussion that immediately follows is indebted to Wilson, *Pulpit in Parliament*, and Hugh R. Trevor-Roper, "The Fast Sermons of the Long Parliament," in *The Crisis of the Seventeenth Century: Religion, the Reformation, and Social Change* (New York: Harper & Row, 1968), 294–344.

politics. Indeed, parliamentary rhetoric became a rebel strong-hold in the English civil war of words, articulating in popular religious terms previously unimaginable events such as revolution and even regicide. In what follows, I analyze primarily the formal humiliations that accompanied monthly fasts instituted by the House of Commons February 23, 1642, as a direct response to the Irish crisis. Strictly defined, this class includes 129 published sermons rightly considered by Walzer, Hugh Trevor-Roper, and John F. Wilson "a basic instrumentality" of the Puritan revolution.[7] And from their inception in the test sacrament of 1614, sermons to Parliament were preoccupied with passivity and its implications: obedience and authority, humiliation and reform.

Introduced by Sir James Perrott to the second Jacobean Parliament, the test sacrament and accompanying sermon gave passivity physical expression. Against the background of the Guy Fawkes Powder Plot and persistent recusant sentiment within England, Perrott motioned on April 9, 1614, that "all the Members may, before a certain Day, receive the Communion." Three reasons were given for this proposal: first, to strengthen the bond between King and Commons, second, to free from suspicion those who would take communion, and, finally, to force Romanists either to reveal their allegiance by disqualifying themselves or to engage in hypocrisy (Wilson, 23–24). In short, the test sacrament compelled certain members of Parliament to eat their words, others to submit to the crown in a physical act of loyalty spun by a preacher whom we must presume was hired for the occasion by the House Speaker. But loyalty, ultimately, to whom? The test sacrament for the following parliament accompanied by the first recorded exhortation and the first general fast (glossed later by John Preston as "Humiliation," "Reconciliation," and "Reformation"; Wilson, 30) show just how

---

7. For a helpful breakdown of major and minor classes of sermons to Parliament, see Wilson, *Pulpit in Parliament*, 7–9, and appendixes. Wilson attests that "in the perspective of corporate piety, the regular as well as the extraordinary humiliations and the thanksgivings—and also the work of the Assembly of Divines—were the basic instrumentalities of the 'puritan revolution'" (189).

slippery obedience can be, especially when ultimate majesty is in dispute. Administration of the sacrament was construed, according to Wilson, not only as a religious test of loyalty applied to the members of Parliament but also as an opportunity to bring the whole body under the discipline of preaching. And in this capacity, reception of the sacrament was deeply subversive to the Crown. In 1623 Isaac Bargrave articulates a theme that was to become highly significant in sermons to the rebellious Long Parliament: the character of Parliament as representative of England before God. "Yee now [re]present the whole body of the Land," Bargrave admonishes, "and therefore now before you approach the *Altar*, Repent for the whole body of the Land" (Wilson, 28). In other words, a test sacrament need not prove the loyalty of parliamentarians to the crown alone, it could in fact do precisely the opposite: prove loyalty of the nation to God *in spite of* intrusions from the Crown. No wonder Bargrave's sermon found considerable disfavor at Court (Wilson, 28). By the time Charles I agreed to a program of monthly humiliations throughout the kingdom, including regular exhortations of the House of Commons, the institution was already far beyond the King's control. Indeed, by agreeing to this system, "Charles I had put into the hands of his enemies a means of coordination and propaganda to which he himself had no parallel" (Trevor-Roper, 306). But contrary to the virile activism Walzer identifies, this political movement and propaganda took the distinct form of a feminized humiliation.

In a sermon preached to the House of Commons on February 23, 1641, Edmund Calamy urges parliamentarians "to be humbled, and ashamed, and broken in heart before the Lord." "It is no signe of an effeminate man," Calamy reassures his auditors, "but of a penitent man to weep this day."[8] October 26, 1642, Thomas Temple preaches to much the same audience about "the

---

8. Edmund Calamy, "God's Free Mercy to England" (London: Meredith, 1642), 2, 23.

honourableness of this subjection to Christ."[9] July 28, 1648, the preeminent clerical politician Stephen Marshall preaches to the Commons about "The Sinne of Hardness of the Heart: The Nature, Danger, and Remedy of it." Therein Marshall condemns the hard hearted for their "disobedience," "willfulnesse," and "obstinacy," chastising that they "stop their ears," "refuse to hearken," and "pull away their shoulders"—like a Beast that refuses to be yoked.[10] Indeed, one of Walzer's favorite activists, John Preston, established as far back as 1625 the form later fast sermons would take in a treatise that seems to be about anything but activism, called *The Saints Qualification: or, a treatise I. Of Humiliation, in Tenne Sermons. II. Of Sanctification, in Nine Sermons. Whereunto is added a Treatise of Communion with Christ in the Sacrament.* . . . As the long title of his treatise already suggests, Preston is interested not only in *imitatio Christi*, or how to imitate Christ by performing good works, but also in *unio Christi*, or "how to take Christ" and become a new creature: "thou doest beleeve that *God* offers his Son unto thee, and thou art willing to take him, not as a Saviour only . . . but as a King to bee subject to him, not as a friend only, but as an husband. . . . When thou doest all this from a love unto him, thou art a *New Creature*."[11] Puritans with varying degrees of conviction thus converged upon what Edmund Calamy called "the very quintessence of Practicall Divinity": England as the new Israel would require new creatures humiliated for collective sins past and reformed for the time to come.[12] Sacred rhetoric would provide the impetus to turn people upside-down, and "man's" feminine soul would provide the frame.

Now I should point out that this topos of the bridal soul was in no way invented by English Nonconformists. We see it, for

9. Thomas Temple, "Christ's Government in and over His People" (London: Gellibrand, 1642), 38.

10. Stephen Marshall, "The Sinne of Hardness of the Heart: The Nature, Danger, and Remedy of it" (London: Cotes, 1648), 5.

11. John Preston, *The Saints Qualification* (London: Bourne, 1637), 345–46.

12. Calamy, "England's looking-glasse" (London: Raworth, 1642), 16.

instance, in Hosea 2.19–20 and in Origen's commentary on *The Song of Songs*, revived by Martin Luther and radicalized by the second-wave German reformer Sebastian Franck—one of the so-called Continental mystics translated and put to use by English radicals in the 1640s and 1650s.[13] Here Franck expresses the feminine virtue of passivity in graphic terms:

> If I let hands and feet droop, despair in myself . . . cling to and squeeze myself, totally resigned under God and surrender to his almighty work which works in me, courts me and desires to impregnate me, and if I surrender—like Mary—that it might do with me according to its will, suffer patiently and without will, I shall instantly be clothed, overshadowed, slept with and impregnated by the power from on high. Then Christ shall be born in those pure brides, as he has been conceived. Thus a rebirth has taken place [*Dies verändert die Natur*] and it alone justifies and cleanses us.[14]

And we should recall as well twice-born-again John Donne's *Holy Sonnets* of 1609, a famous formulation that characteristically pushes the metaphor of seduction to its dramatic extreme: "Take me to you, imprison me, for I / Except you enthral me, never shall be free / Nor ever chaste, you ravish me." Indeed, in the religious context at least, Walzer's new creature "self-confident and free of worry, capable of vigorous, willful activity" (313) is nowhere to be found. Instead, the person reborn into a godly commonwealth is the product of humiliation, anxiety, and soulful, feminine passivity, in the best sense of the word.

So was this revolution in any sense a kind of conscious activism or modern self-assertion directed against the Crown? Perhaps secondarily so, in the sense of "activism" familiar to the revolutionary saints from Roman republican sources and their Renaissance commentators. But we can already see that, in this important parliamentary context, radical reform was conceived

13. Nigel Smith, *Perfection Proclaimed: Language and Literature in English Radical Religion 1640–1660* (Oxford: Clarendon Press, 1989), 105–226.

14. Sebastian Franck, *280 Paradoxes or Wondrous Sayings*, trans. E. J. Furcha (Lewiston, NY: Mellen, 1986), 414–15.

first in religious terms that ran directly counter to a program of classical republican activism. Reform was not in any way conceived, say, as the assertion of individual and corporate rights against the Crown, or even as a defense of natural law. On the model of personal reformation, national reformation was instead conceived most often as self-sacrifice and passive obedience to God-the-bridegroom. As one of the leading Presbyterian ministers in London, Thomas Case, put it in a sermon on Hosea's "Spirituall Whoredome," a nation or kingdom should rather stand "in a conjugal relation unto God" (Wilson, 169). And if reform meant the emasculation of secular powers both perfidious and pious, then so be it.

In revolutionary England, moreover, the rhetoric of rebirth is no longer just a matter of personal piety. In his immensely popular 1641 sermon "England's looking-glasse," Edmund Calamy asserts, "As the Reformation must be Personall, so also it must be Nationall. . . . A particular man by turning unto God, may turn away a particular Judgment. But when the sins of a Nation are generall, and the Judgments upon a Nation generall, the turning must be generall. . . . There must be a Court-Reformation, a Countrey-Reformation, a City-Reformation, Church and State-Reformation, a Generall Reformation."[15] Decades later, after the Restoration, William Bridge could dramatize this powerful analogy in a synonym by preaching about "Gods Return to the Soul, or Nation."[16] There is, then, a deep continuity between the structure of modern political revolutions and the structure of Christian rebirth sketched in 2 Corinthians 5.17: "Therefore if any man is in Christ, he is a New Creature; the old things passed away; behold the new things have come." And Walzer rightly recognizes this connection between personal and national renovation even beyond the immediate context of the English Civil War when he remarks, "Before Puritans, Jacobins, or Bolsheviks attempt the

15. Edmund Calamy, "England's looking-glasse," 27.
16. William Bridge, "Christ and the Covenant. The Work and Way of Meditation. Gods Return to the Soul, or Nation" (London: Printed for N. Ranew and J. Robinson at the Angel in Jewen-Street, 1667).

creation of a new order, they must create new men" (Walzer, 315).
But to call these revolutionary new creatures self-confident and
free of worry, capable of vigorous, willful activity, as Walzer does,
is a stretch, to say the least, especially in the religious context of the
English Civil War. To understand how certain Enlightenment
sensibilities make it nearly impossible for leftist critics such as
Walzer to articulate the very bond between passivity and reform
that early modern subjects presumed most natural, we must now
move beyond religion to the disciplines that provided techni-
cians of early modern subjectivity the mechanics, so to speak, of
human renovation: natural philosophy and rhetoric—disciplines
similarly prepared to describe and exploit the possibilities of humankind's *second nature*.[17]

The Gender of Human Nature

If we can bracket our effort to find in Reformation doctrine some
proactive techne of the soul—some suggestion as to how grace
can be achieved through force of mind and will—a rich area of
inquiry comes into view: namely, the passive soul and its more
demure habits. Though, as Edmund Calamy laments, it may not
be in the power of a person "to convert himself,"[18] souls could at
least be readied for divine inscription and rendered supple and
receptive to the Holy Spirit. Passivity of the soul would have to
become a kind of ethos, or second nature, and second nature was
a woman. Salvation itself would be impossible without suffering,
and Stoic apathy was condemned even by church doctors such

17. Denied the *Oxford English Dictionary* honor of a citation from an early master
such as Chaucer, Caxton, or even Shakespeare, *nature* remains largely unromantic until
sense number 13 and the era of *Paradise Lost* (1667), when Milton conjures in the image of a female moon "such vast room in Nature unpossest By living Soule." *Paradise
Lost*, 8.153. And not until the nineteenth century do we hear consistently about what
William Cowper calls "unconscious nature" with its rocks, groves, and streams. Before
the scientific revolution, nature was instead rooted in the Latin *nasci*, to be born, denot-
ing thereby some innate quality as in this warning from *Pilgrimage of Perfection* (1526):
"though ye fall neuer so oft by impecyncey, through y' fraylty of nature."

18. Calamy, "England's looking-glasse," 38.

as Bernard and Bonaventure (see chapter 2). Clearly something could be done to ready the soul for divine inscription, but this readiness would not be a matter of sheer will or Stoic reason, as Walzer and other commentators suggest. Quite the opposite, in fact, as William Spurstowe insisted in his 1643 call for a program of fasting more effective in producing "constant humiliation" and a passionate rather than merely rational sorrow.[19] Required was a mode of practiced passivity, the sort of patience and suffering appropriate to "man's" feminized nature.

Scholars have largely overlooked the role that Christian passivity plays in the history of the human sciences, political theory in particular.[20] More attention has been given to the human activity that produces knowledge in the human sciences—a corollary of Vico's principle: *verum et factum convertuntur* (the nature of the true is that it has been made). But when we tease from these parliamentary sermons their forgotten Aristotelian connotations, we find that Christian passivity is necessary to explain how human nature can be moved at all, whether by way of habit (second nature), by divine intervention (supernature), or by both in cooperation. And it is in part my purpose here to suggest that passivity cannot be easily eradicated from projects of human transformation whatever the political end might be.

19. William Spurstowe, "Englands Patterne and Duty In It's Monthly Fasts," quoted in Wilson, *Pulpit in Parliament*, 71–72.

20. Scott Paul Gordon's *The Power of the Passive Self in English Literature, 1640–1770* (Cambridge: Cambridge University Press, 2002) is a notable exception. His study of Protestant writing, acting theory, and sentimental literature traces admirably how the "passivity trope" paradoxically enables actions "that would otherwise be difficult to conceive, from revolutionary action against a monarch to public speaking by women" (17). However, Gordon fails to extend this analysis to the social sciences, where he instead sees a Hobbesian calculation of self-interest prevail over a model of Christian passivity (55). For a counterview, see my article "Melanchthon's Rhetoric" (see chap. 2, n. 15). Others who explore the function of passivity in Protestant writing include Christopher Hill in *God's Englishman: Oliver Cromwell and English Revolution* (New York: Dial, 1970) and especially Phyllis Mack in *Visionary Women: Ecstatic Prophecy in Seventeenth-Century England* (Berkeley: University of California Press, 1992). For a thoughtful theoretical discussion, see Thomas Carl Wall, *Radical Passivity: Levinas, Blanchot, and Agamben* (Albany: SUNY Press, 1999).

It certainly poses no difficulty to find doctrinal statements that flat out reject custom, habit, or usage as aids to supervenient grace. The same John Preston deeply concerned with the practicalities of *The Saints Daily Exercise*[21] could consider grace strictly "artificial" and "infused" when composing a more formal treatise (*Saints Qualification*, 364–65). And based on such unambiguous statements, it seems justified to conclude with Donald Kelley that, for Protestant reformers, second nature was even more corrupt than first.[22] The afterlife of both fallen natures would thus seem to lie not in religious modernity, but rather in secular modernity: "as the fortunes of the idea of nature underlie the history of modern science," Kelley concludes, "the fortunes of the idea of 'second nature' underlie the history of modern social science" (100). However, the second nature that underlies the history of modern social science is in fact continuous with Reformation thought and its legacy in the seventeenth century (here I am using *Reformation* with a capital *R*). To understand how this is so, we must look to the tradition of Aristotelian physics and return, specifically, to the passions.

When we speak in one breath of moving the passions, patience, and suffering, we tap into Aristotelian thought in its English form. Aristotle discusses how mover and moved can be distinguished by employing the example of teacher and student. Although there can be no motion in the abstract—for example, no teaching outside of the relationship between A and B—one can still make a discursive distinction between agent and patient, action and passion (like saying that the road from Thebes to Athens is the same as that from Athens to Thebes, while distinguishing between the two by way of quality).[23] The point relevant to my

21. John Preston, *The Saints Daily Exercise. A Treatise concerning the whole dutie of prayer* (London: Bourne, 1629).

22. Donald R. Kelley, "*Altera natura*: The Idea of Custom in Historical Perspective," in *New Perspectives on Renaissance Thought: Essays in the History of Science, Education and Philosophy*, ed. John Henry and Sarah Hutton (London: Duckworth, 1990), 97.

23. Aristotle, *Physics*, 202a23–202b8. For an excellent discussion of how action, passion, and *motus* are confounded in early modern interpretations of Aristotle, see Dennis

discussion is that for Aristotle, activity remains sheer potential if it lacks a subject. There can be no building without a buildable, no healing without a healable, no teaching without the teachable, no agency without "patience," no action without "passion." For Aristotle, the very definition of motion demands tractability, and tractability can be broken down into various forms of passion. The passions of the inanimate and of nonrational living beings (which aren't emotions in the strict sense) occupy the *Physics*, the *Parts of Animals*, *Of Generation and Corruption*; the passions unique to humans are described in the *Rhetoric*, *Ethics*, and *Politics*.

Passions, patience, and suffering are for Aristotle much more than nominal qualities of a blank slate. They always express a kind of potential.[24] Whence this potential? In the case of bronze, its potential to become a statue lies at the juncture of its natural substance and the motivating end imposed from without—namely, the intentions of the sculptor. But in the case of a student, the potential to learn is more than just a natural capacity met by the motivating intentions of a teacher. Over and above nature lies the critical domain of humanity that since Shakespeare's *Tempest* we have called "nurture." A pedagogical commonplace developed in the rhetorical tradition suggests that, without habituation, natural capacity comes to naught (for even the gifted orator must practice speaking). With habit, however, nature can be enhanced, or even superseded. Indeed, the consequences of nurture can be stunning, as a notorious passage from the pseudo-Aristotelian *Problems* reveals. The sexually graphic passage that follows is ironically *locus classicus* for the patristic commonplace that "habit is second nature," and it is worth citing at length. It is also classic condemnation of feminine passivity that helps explain

---

Des Chene, "Motus, Potentia, Actus," chapter 2 of *Physiologia: Natural Philosophy in Late Aristotelian and Cartesian Thought* (Ithaca, NY: Cornell University Press, 1996).

24. A point that has been elaborated in detail by Susan James in *Passion and Action* (see chap. 1, n. 1).

just how radical it was when early Christians and later reformers would sing its praises:

> But the naturally effeminate are so circumstanced that little or no secretion occurs in the place in which it occurs with normal persons, but is secreted in this region (i.e., the fundament). The reason is that such persons are unnaturally constituted; for though they are male this part of them has become maimed. Such maiming produces either complete destruction or a distortion of type. The former is impossible in their case for it would imply their becoming female. So it must involve distortion and an impulse in some direction other than discharge of semen. So they are unsatisfied, like women; for the moisture is slight and does not force an exit and is quickly chilled. Those with whom the semen travels to the fundament desire to be passive, and those with whom it settles in both places desire to be both active and passive in sexual intercourse; in whichever direction it inclines the more, so do their desires. In some cases this state is the result of habit. For men are accustomed to enjoy what they normally do, and to emit semen accordingly. So they desire to do that by which this may occur and so habit tends to become second nature [*ethos hesper physis ginetai*]. For this reason those who have not been accustomed to submit to sexual intercourse before puberty but at about that time, because they have recollection of their enjoyment and pleasure is associated with the recollection, because of their habit desire the passive state, as if it were natural, numerous occasions and habit having the same effect as nature. If a man happens to be both lustful and effeminate, this is all the more likely to occur.[25]

Besides the quaint hydraulics, what fascinates in this passage is the complex and even paradoxical treatment of the nature/nurture problem. First, nature can be naturally perturbed: a man can be unnaturally constituted and thus tend toward feminine sexual habits while maintaining his masculine type. Bodily fluids and

25. Pseudo-Aristotle, *Problems*, 6.26, trans. W. S. Hett and H. Rackham (Cambridge, MA: Harvard University Press, 1937); a set of texts spuriously attributed to Aristotle, originating perhaps from his field notes and significantly revised by others as late as the fifth or sixth century AD.

their distribution determine the contours of desire: those in whom semen travels to the fundament desire to be passive, and those in whom it settles in both fundament and genitalia desire to be both active and passive, and so on. However, "feminine nature" seems to be an empty category, a category of lack in what Thomas Laqueur would call a single-sex species.[26] At one point, the female is hypothetically defined as negative antithesis to the male. If the male type were completely destroyed, what one would be left with is simply a female. Women are *un*satisfied because their moisture is slight, does not force an exit, and is quickly chilled. Passivity is unequivocally established as antithesis to activity. It is a kind of dulled second nature that weakly imitates the first, and it is most certainly gendered female.

But here the story starts to complicate. With pleasure, practice, and memory, not only can seemingly natural desires be permanently transformed, but so can the very hydraulics that provide nature its medium. Men are accustomed to enjoy what they normally do, and emit semen accordingly. But what do men normally do? That is a question impossible for the author of this passage to answer in universal terms. What we do know is that whatever one normally does will tend to become second nature. If reinforced over time, *nomos* becomes *physis*; or as Aristotle himself phrases it in the *Nicomachean Ethics*: "I say that habit's but long practice, friend, And this becomes men's nature in the end" (1152a25–35). And there is a further complication. In the *Problems*, nature itself seems to be gendered male and couched in terms of active desire. Second nature seems to be gendered female and couched in terms of a passive desire that eventually maims and destroys its male host.

In any case, we see in the *Problems* a deep anxiety about the fragile status of nature. Given in its essence, nature is nonetheless susceptible to corruption at its very core. And this inherent fragility of nature, I argue, would be reinscribed after

---

26. Thomas Laqueur, *Making Sex: Body and Gender from the Greeks to Freud* (Cambridge, MA: Harvard University Press, 1990).

the Reformation in positive terms, when civic leaders such as
Edmund Calamy, Thomas Coleman, Thomas Temple, Stephen
Marshall, and John Preston demanded that "Nature itself [be]
altered: Lion [turned] into Lamb."[27] This turn, moreover, is
critical. For rather than worry about nature's fragility, reforming Christians from Luther and Calvin to the English Nonconformists *exploit* fragility as a precondition to grace. In the words
of Thomas Coleman, "A tractablenesse of heart must be a forerunner of the receipt of the benefit."[28] Indeed, a number of these
revolutionary saints follow John Preston by casting the "tractablenesse of heart" in surprisingly naturalistic terms adopted both
from Aristotelian physics and the new critical philosophies of
Francis Bacon and René Descartes. Much like the introspective
Descartes of the *Meditations*, Preston asks his auditors in *The
Saints Qualification* first to "looke on your owne natures, your
owne errours, the secret windings, and turnings of the heart, your
owne thoughts and affections, and see what a disproportion, a dis-
likenesse there is" (33). This done, one will be compelled to admit
that "The nature of man is full of all Unrighteousnesse," indeed
the very faculties of humankind are corrupt. In the following ten
sermons on humiliation, Preston then enumerates precisely what
faculties are corrupt and in what ways. He treats in order "The
corruption of the Understanding, in five things," "The corruption
of the Memory, in two things," "The corruption of the Conscience, in three acts of it," "The corruption of the sensitive
appetite," and finally, the most problematic, "corruption of the
Affections." "Either they are not active," Preston explains of the
affections, "not placed where they should be, or if they be placed
where they should be, they are ready to runne over, to over-love,
and over-grieve, and over-joy" (32–63). Finally, Preston specifies
that the radical transformation of the faculties accomplished by
the New Creature is not substantial but "dispositional": "The

27. Preston, *Saints Qualification*, 363.
28. Thomas Coleman, "The Christian Course and Complaint" (London: Meredith,
1643), 14.

meaning is not, that the substance of a man is changed, but the order and frame of his soule is altered, there are the same strings, as it were, but there is a new tune put to them" (324). Not surprisingly, this "new tune" is infused by God in two acts: "perswasion and then resolution" (439).

Almost twenty years later, on July 28, 1648, Stephen Marshall would pick up this curious theme in his sermon to Parliament on "The Sinne of Hardness of the Heart: The Nature, Danger, and Remedy of it": the very flesh of humankind is subject to a kind of verbal persuasion. "This same fleshy heart," Marshall proclaims, "is a heart upon which Gods seale leaves a print, Gods counsell I meane, his Word, threatenings, exhortations, or whatsoever comes from him leaves a stampe upon him; It is a heart that is wax to God, willing to bee moulded, resignes up it selfe to bee to God what God would have it to bee" (29). Though ever susceptible to evil impressions, passive dispositions emerge in this revolutionary discourse as the key to overcoming a nature thoroughly corrupt. Obviously hesitant to adopt the mundane discourse of second nature already well-developed in the practical disciplines of moral philosophy, pedagogy, and rhetoric, radical theologians did prefer the language of supernatural infusion when discussing in doctrinal terms the fountainhead of grace. But when it came to the mechanics of rebirth, these same theologians would often take refuge in a more practical language that offered its subjects guidance in how rebirth might feel, how it might be effected, and ultimately how one might prepare for it by carefully exercising the soul *away* from its nature.

When natural terms are revalued, gender terms are revalued as well. Now a feminine passivity that facilitates the soul's inscription is encouraged, and willful, masculine activity discouraged, as in John Milton's diatribe against masculine tyranny *Eikonoklastes*.[29] Indeed, what appears to be "man's" fallen nature would

---

29. "And if it hath bin anciently interpreted the presaging signe of a future Tyrant, but to dream of copulation with his Mother, what can it be less than actual Tyranny to affirme waking, that the Parlament, which is his Mother, can neither conceive or bring.

be reinscribed by good habits to a second nature gendered female. In early seventeenth-century England, for instance, innumerable tracts were written and sermons preached on "the saint's daily exercise": prayer, rigorous introspection, and so forth. Starting, then, with original nature and following the suggested allegory to its logical conclusion, the sequence of human development in biblical time would be feminine → masculine → feminine, the middle span perfectly coinciding with the duration of "man's" lapse.

It is worth noting, moreover, that this particular gender reversal has been overlooked by feminist studies of science that too easily conflate natures human and nonhuman, in the process reifying the very male/female, active/passive dyads I, and presumably they, wish to deconstruct. For instance, Carolyn Merchant typically sacrifices subtlety for polemic force when she flatly asserts in her 1980 academic best-seller *The Death of Nature: Women, Ecology and the Scientific Revolution* that, between the sixteenth and seventeenth centuries, "the image of an organic cosmos with a living female earth at its center gave way to a mechanistic worldview in which nature was reconstructed as dead and passive, to be dominated and controlled by humans."[30] Neatly articulated, the

---

forth *any authoritative Act* without his Masculine coition." John Milton, *Eikonoklastes*, in *Works of John Milton*, vol. 5, ed. William Haller (New York: Columbia University Press, 1932), 186.

30. Carolyn Merchant, *The Death of Nature: Women, Ecology and the Scientific Revolution* (San Francisco: Harper & Row, 1980), xvi. In *Counterrevolution and Revolt* (Boston: Beacon Press, 1972), Marcuse is careful to distinguish between forms of nature when he asks, "What is involved in the liberation of nature as a vehicle of the liberation of man? This notion refers to (1) *human* nature: man's primary impulses and senses as foundation of his rationality and experience and (2) *external* nature: man's existential environment, the 'struggle with nature' in which he forms his society" (59). Later, Marcuse clarifies how this revolutionary process is gendered: "The faculty of being 'receptive,' 'passive,' is a precondition of freedom: it is the ability to see things in their own right, to experience the joy enclosed in them, the erotic energy of nature—an energy which is there to be liberated; nature, too, awaits the revolution! This receptivity is itself the soil of creation: it is opposed, not to productivity, but to *destructive* productivity. The latter has been the ever more conspicuous feature of male domination; inasmuch as the 'male principle' has been the ruling mental and physical force, a free society would be the 'definite negation' of this principle—it would be a *female* society" (74–75).

destructive transformation would then be just as neatly reversed at the level of ideology according to Merchant, masculine technological culture replaced by something like Herbert Marcuse's female society. Even Lorraine Daston makes the analogous reductive move in her generally outstanding 1992 article "The Naturalized Female Intellect," when she simplifies the contrast for the sake of clarity: "early modern nature was benevolent, purposeful, and sovereign through enlightened assent; modern nature was indifferent, aimless, and sovereign through physical necessity."[31] The effort to deconstruct nature's essence thus tends to founder on a prejudice of our post-Enlightenment age: it is erroneously assumed by a range of feminist critics from Simone de Beauvoir to Daston that, for all intents and purposes, nature in a Christian sense expired in early modernity with the rise of normal science. With this assumption firmly in place, feminist critics of science thereby overlook a powerful articulation of the sort I have thus far described in Christian humanist discourse, human science, and beyond.

Considering nature from the perspective of human science rather than natural science and from the perspective of rhetoric rather than philosophy yields fresh insight. For we learn that early modern science in the broadest sense was burdened with contrary impulses scholars have not adequately considered, let alone reconciled. Whereas we have been told that Bacon's virile science was designed to master the external threat posed by mother nature, scholars have largely overlooked the fact that, in contrast, early modern *human* science was designed to mobilize "man's" feminine soul for broadly political purposes—again as the influential Puritan divine John Preston put it "nature itself" would be altered in the creation of new creatures suitable for a godly commonwealth, lion turned into lamb. In other words, two different sciences, two different natures. And not surprisingly, a new and politically motivated interest in the mobility of souls

31. Lorraine Daston, "The Naturalized Female Intellect," *Science in Context* 5, no. 2 (1992): 222.

catalyzed a rearticulation of gender as well, exacerbating and finally institutionalizing what Debora Shuger has called the "crisis of manhood" represented in the Calvinist passion narratives of an earlier period.[32] This crisis, we should note, was institutionalized only insofar as it became an explicit mode of political discourse per Robert Filmer's *Patriarcha*.[33] By no means, however, were gender positions thereby set in stone. Masculinity and femininity, I wish to emphasize, are invertible discursive positions that *constitute* rather than *express* radically different subject positions: obedient to the king, for instance, and suspicious of Parliament (Filmer's identification with the king-as-patriarch), rebellious toward the king and obedient to God (Milton's ambivalent identification with the virgin mother), passive toward the self and active in the community (the Calvinist hermaphrodite), prideful and vainglorious, or abject and humiliated. It is, moreover, this very fluidity that makes gender an indispensable trope when political subjectivity itself is in flux.

Needless to say, then, a logic of gender reversal that subordinates man to woman was not applied uniformly in post-Reformation thought or consistently worked out in any particular theology. If told explicitly, the story usually took shape as one might expect, casting Eve both as the agent of man's fall from grace and the patient overcome by man's renovation. Feminine passivity—constructed of course from the masculine perspective—could never be comfortably embraced by men petrified by "effeminacy," as the vicious satires of "Mistris Parliament" reveal.[34] For that matter, the story of salvation could also be told as

32. Debora Kuller Shuger, *The Renaissance Bible: Scholarship, Sacrifice, and Subjectivity* (Berkeley: University of California Press, 1994), 116–22. See also Michael C. Schoenfeldt, *Prayer and Power: George Herbert and Renaissance Courtship* (Chicago: University of Chicago Press, 1991); Mark Breitenberg, *Anxious Masculinity in Early Modern England* (Cambridge: Cambridge University Press, 1996); Richard Rambuss *Closet Devotions* (Durham, NC: Duke University Press, 1998).

33. Robert Filmer, *"Patriarcha" and Other Writings*, ed. Johann P. Sommerville (Cambridge: Cambridge University Press, 1991).

34. See, for instance, Mercurius Melancholicus, "Mistris Parliament Brought to Bed of a Monstrous Childe of Reformation" (1648). As the work of feminist critics from Luce

a homoerotic romance complete with the hesitations of a tender courtship, the melancholy of love, and the final ecstasy of consummation. "There is a most sweet soul-ravishing intimacy and bosome familiarity that passeth between Christ and his people," observes John Langley in "Gemitus Columbae: The Mournfull Note of the Dove," a sermon preached at Margaret's Westminster before the House of Commons December 25, 1644.[35] In Langley's quaint interpretation, *The Song of Solomon* "shews what sweet billings, flutterings, and embracings do passe between them [Christ and his lover], what walks they do take together in the gallery, what refreshing in the Wine-seller." But this sentimental courtship soon gives way to more explosive passion: "Hence those ravishments and springings of spirit sometimes in Gods Children, as in master *Glover* at the stake, he cries out, *He is come, He is come*" (5–6). In a similar vein, John Preston observed that a man "loves a man truly . . . when thou doest finde thy heart so humbled, that thou doest reckon sinne the greatest evill, and doest hunger after Christ, and doest keep him as thy life." And "when thou doest all this from a love unto him," Preston concludes, "thou art a New Creature."[36]

In the end, a scheme that lends itself to calling the "naturally" effeminate male "unnatural" will never cater to the cause of consistency. However, when we give this Aristotelian scheme a genealogy and take it to a logical conclusion, we gain new insight into the process by which human nature was engendered in early modernity. Rather than simply the product of a new calculus of

---

Irigaray and Evelyn Fox Keller to Mary Sheriff and Judith Butler suggests, this discursive gambit is perhaps better described as a masculine appropriation of woman's generative capacity, or even the expression of masculine melancholy that comes with the foreclosure of the feminine. See Evelyn Fox Keller, "Baconian Science: The Arts of Mastery and Obedience," in *Reflections on Gender and Science* (New Haven, CT: Yale University Press, 1985); Mary D. Sheriff, "Passionate Spectators: Enthusiasm, Nymphomania, and the Imagined Tableau," in *Enthusiasm and Enlightenment in Europe, 1650–1850*, ed. Lawrence E. Klein and Anthony J. La Vopa (San Marino, CA: Huntington Library, 1998), 51–84.

35. John Langley, "Gemitus Columbae: The Mournfull Note of the Dove" (London: Stephens, 1644).

36. Preston *Saints Qualification*, 346.

self-interest (Albert Hirschman's thesis), human nature in the seventeenth century was the product of a science designed to master the physics of passivity in all of its gender trouble. What deserved scrutiny was not simply our depraved natural desires and inclinations, but rather the dynamics of susceptibility: how we listen and learn, emote and reform. And this is why rhetoric assumed an important position in post-Reformation doctrine and practice, for the rhetorical tradition had established in fine detail the mechanics of speech situations, pedagogy, and motions of the soul.

Returning to the immediate historical object, I can now better show what the consequences are when Puritan divines cast rhetorical susceptibility in the metanarrative of collective sin and redemption. "Oh the divine Rhetorick, and omnipotent efficacies of Repentance!" exclaimed Edmund Calamy as he worked upon parliamentarians' hearts and affections, constructing with divine eloquence "England's looking-glasse"(15). In "The Church Sinking, Saved by Christ" (February 26, 1644) Simeon Ash considers Jesus Christ "a perfect patterne to persuade,"[37] thereby subordinating the superficial rhetoric of schoolmen and enthusiasts to the fundamental rhetoric of Christ. But it is Joseph Caryl's "England's Plus Ultra" that gives us the clearest understanding of rhetoric's critical role in revolutionary practice, theorizing in explicit terms how history, rhetoric, and religion are intimately bound.

The occasional nature of Caryl's sermon is evident in its long title: "England's Plus Ultra, Both of hoped Mercies, and of Required Duties: Shewed in a Sermon Preached to the honorable houses of Parliament, the Lord Major, Court of Aldermen, and Common-councell of London, together with the Assembly of Divines, at Christ Church, April 1, 1646. Being their day of publike Thanksgiving to Almighty God for the great success of the Parliaments Army in the West, especially in Cornwall, under the

---

37. Simeon Ash, "The Church Sinking, Saved by Christ" (London: Brewster, 1645), A2r.

Conduct of his Excellency Sir Thomas Fairfax."[38] For Caryl there is no such thing as a simple chronicle of events in either a holy war or a war against personal sin. Instead, one must negotiate "a five-fold declaration of the works of God," five ways, in other words, to characterize events: arithmetically, logically, theologically, historically, and rhetorically. Rhetorical declaration, Caryl explains, is when "besides a bare narrative of facts, &c. (which is proper to history) we labour to find out the severall circumstances and aggravations of every work which may raise up our spirits, and warm our hearts in considering of, and look over them" (27–29). In other words it would be hard-hearted if an event such as the success of Fairfax's army in Cornwall were recounted as simple fact. Simple chronicle events must be "aggravated" to the point that they cross the threshold from reason to passion, acceding thereby to the metanarrative of collective sin and redemption inscribed ultimately by God in the heart of humankind. Rhetoric makes a difference down to the very word. "For as it is not enough to make an *Arithmeticall confession* of sins," continues Caryl, "or to make an *historicall declaration of them*, to set down the time and place, when and where we sinned; but it is our duty to make rhetoricall confessions, to aggravate our sinnes against ourselves, to shew the Lord not only our sinne, but the iniquity of our sinne, the filthinesse of our lewdnesse, the abomination of our provocations" (30). Just as a military encounter requires what we call spin to become a victory for God, the events of our lives require a rhetorical context to be meaningful: before it is put in emotional terms, before it is "lewd" and "abominable," it can hardly be called a sin. As even the skeptical Thomas Hobbes admits in *Leviathan*, without the passion that gives language a home, humans are condemned to lives of poor judgment and dull indifference.

>>><<<

The passive soul is thus precondition to all sorts of change, whether religious or secular. It is the object of God's will and thus

---

38. Joseph Caryl, "England's Plus Ultra" (London: Rothwell, 1646).

the subject of theology, or the object of human science and the subject of secular rhetoric. However, the passive soul is anything but conducive to the natural science that emerged in England at the same time. In fact, I will conclude this chapter by reading the passive soul as *bête noire* to Francis Bacon's experimental philosophy. Suddenly, one of the most notorious metaphors in the Western canon takes on new meaning—this from Bacon's *New Organon*: "For as yet we are but lingering in the outer courts of nature, nor are we preparing ourselves a way into her inner chambers. Yet no one can endow a given body with a new nature, or successfully and aptly transmute it into a new body, unless he has attained a competent knowledge of the body so to be altered or transformed."[39] To subject nature to our will and transform it, in other words, one must first solicit nature's latent capacities. Bacon's is thus a method, and a metaphor, that turns nature on its head. Or should I say *her* head? If we compare this passage to Preston's term by term, we discover that each term has been methodically displaced. In both cases, nature would be disciplined and transformed. But where Preston has "man's" hyperactive internal nature rendered a feminine receptacle for the seed of God's wisdom, Bacon subjects a wildly feminine external nature to the penetrating gaze of a knowledge gendered male. In Preston's image, we would all become bridesmaid to God's penetrating Word; in Bacon's, we would all become perpetrator. Finally, for Preston and the English reformers, *Rhetorica* is a key to knowledge; for Bacon, she is the demise of knowledge.

Common parlance today would suggest that Bacon's rough treatment of feminine nature became a dominant trope in Western modernity instead of the Reformation trope of "man's" fallen nature refeminized. But when we analyze human nature in seventeenth-century political rhetoric—indeed, in the emerging human sciences generally—we discover a much more

---

39. Francis Bacon, *The New Organon: Or True Directions concerning the Interpretation of Nature* (1620) in *Francis Bacon: A Selection of His Works*, ed. Sidney Warhaft (New York: Macmillan, 1982), 382.

complicated story, one that challenges the Frankfurt School thesis that technological modernity and aggressive masculinity go hand in hand. If natural science now carries the burden of masculine hyperactivism identified by the likes of Marcuse and Keller, human science carries the burden of a passivism responsible at the same time for the worst kind of social engineering and the best kind of social reform. Passivity's double-edged sword was, in fact, sharpened in the Age of Reason—not dulled, as Walzer and others would have it—and it continues to cut through the rhetoric of the human sciences blindly, leaving a diminished political life in its path. We face on one hand the legacy of a post-1960s activism unable to articulate at what great expense political subjects are produced, on the other a postmodernism so sensitive to this expense that a new incapacity develops: postmodern sensibilities make it difficult to reconcile decentered subjectivity with political agency, passivism with activism. This chapter has been designed in part to deconstruct the false paradox of postmodernism by showing, first, that political subjectivity was originally conceived in Civil War England as the very marriage of a decentered or "humiliated" subjectivity with political agency, passivism toward the self with activism toward the community. So "Good men are Publicke Goods Actively, as well as Passively," preached a member of the Assembly of Divines, Daniel Cawdry, to the House of Commons January 31, 1643: "That is, men of publicke Spirits, active for the publicke Good, though passive in neglect of themselves."[40] Dissolving the radical passive/active opposition clears space we need in order to see how early modern emotion and the economy of scarcity works in more detail: we can now see better how pride and humility are differential emotions that can be mobilized politically, with the apparently "active" vice of pride condemned for its ineffectiveness and the "passive" virtue of humility serving the most dramatic revolutionary ends. Once again we see how emotions are not essentially universal traits of our

---

40. Daniel Cawdry, "The Good Man a Publick Good, 1. Passively, 2. Actively" (London: Greene, 1643), 25.

biology expressed by individuals, but are, rather, contested terms negotiated in a public sphere where power is distributed unevenly. Next, I will show how reading emotions such as pride and humility as contested terms revitalizes the literature of sensibility. This approach allows us to better read both a philosophical text like David Hume's *Treatise of Human Nature* and a sentimental novel like Sarah Fielding's *David Simple* as cultural artifacts that instantiate social passions, rather than merely describing them poorly.

4

The Politics of Pride in
David Hume and *David Simple*

In the act of self-constitution that David Hume describes in *A Treatise of Human Nature* (1740), the soul is revealed in its basic vulnerability. For the very passions such as love and hate, pride and humility that constitute personal identity turn out to be political in the most literal sense, woven as they are in particular relations of "government and subordination." So what exactly are the politics of pride and humility according to Hume? How do pride and humility map onto available regimes of government and subordination? Answering these questions helps us historicize particular forms of self in the eighteenth-century culture of sensibility and, as I hope to demonstrate via Sarah Fielding's novel *David Simple* (1744), help us read its literature. Reading sentimental literature at this point is helpful if we wish to understand the politics of emotion, because its formal success depends upon negotiating emotion in what I have been calling a political "economy of scarcity." After all, writing as if emotions are essentially divorced from circumstance and distributed symmetrically by nature would make for a boring narrative indeed. What we consider a successful novel often depends upon portraying in compelling fashion how emotions—unevenly distributed—are negotiated across circumstance and character (a process ending in what the Romance Writers of America suggestively call "emotional justice"). Finally, reading Fielding against Hume reminds us that an emotion such as pride is not the exclusive property of the powerful in the economy of emotional scarcity, but is rather a contested term subject to reappropriation by the relatively powerless: think, for instance, of the function "gay pride" has today.

In broad terms, this chapter is about the emergence of specific complementary and gendered selves in the English culture of sensibility, and the consequent demise of passivity as a public virtue. Crucial to this critical intellectual history is my focus on the discipline psychology as a rhetorical art originally designed to *transform* psyche by way of the passions, rather than describe and categorize psyche in the mode of late-modern natural science.

Hume's Republic of the Soul

"Of all crimes that human creatures are capable of committing," ventures Hume in *A Treatise of Human Nature*, "the most horrid and unnatural is ingratitude."[1] This might seem to us an overstatement, even when we consider that Hume shares this harsh evaluation with Seneca and Cicero and that he immediately raises the cardinal example of ingratitude committed against parents and ending in injury or death. Of course, the Judeo-Christian tradition does consider milder forms of ingratitude (as in the story of the ten healed lepers, only one of whom returned to thank Jesus) regrettable, but certainly not a sin of the same order as denying God or taking an innocent life. And though it may be unbecoming played out on the public stage—like a wealthy athlete holding out in contract negotiations—ingratitude in our secular culture will more likely land one in the pages of the *New York Post* than in jail. Indeed, it might be this sort of overheated

---

1. David Hume, *A Treatise of Human Nature*, ed. David Fate Norton and Mary J. Norton (Oxford: Oxford University Press, 2000), 300.

enthusiasm that compels editors to leave out the *Treatise*'s second book, "Of the Passions," entirely when abridging Hume's most substantial work for the sake of serious philosophy.[2] So why for Hume is ingratitude so horrid and unnatural? Answering this question unlocks the premises of Hume's philosophy of the passions and thereby provides one key to the culture of sensibility in which Hume played a formative role.

What would be left of Hume's generous man if gratitude owed him remained terminally unpaid? Would something like integrity be left—the self-assurance that comes with knowledge that one leads a good life despite the ingratitude of one's family or friends, colleagues or acquaintances? Or perhaps the promise of reward in the afterlife that might give meaning to the life of a Christian martyr? In fact, what would be left for Hume is precisely nothing: assurance would have no self to speak of, knowledge would have no object, and integrity would have nothing to integrate. Even the retroactive fiction of the Christian martyr-to-be would be insufficient to constitute a Humean self, because the chain of association from benevolent action to ultimate reward would be tenuous without some sort of human appreciation in this world. Even Jesus had his apostles, after all.

Let us consider why Humean self-assurance would be impossible either in isolation or where all subject positions were equal, which amounts to the same thing. What would it mean, first of all, for the self to depend upon gratitude in its very constitution? It would mean there would be no self without recognition by a particular other, without some sort of acknowledgment that says "there you are with respect to me." In other words, gratitude constitutes something more than a Lacanian subject whose sense of a unified self emerges out of a universal experience of misrecognition and self-objectification in the Mirror Stage; it constitutes a *particular* self in a particular relation of power to another who is there, *Da*, positioned in a particular way. Gratitude, for instance,

2. See, for instance, David Hume, *On Human Nature and the Understanding*, ed. Antony Flew (New York: Collier, 1962).

bolsters the prince more readily than the pauper. Or as Hume puts it in one of his ethical thought experiments: "'Tis evident, that tho' all passions pass easily from one object to another related to it, yet this transition is made with greater facility, where the more considerable object is first presented, and the lesser follows it, than when this order is revers'd, and the lesser takes precedence. Thus 'tis more natural for us to love the son upon account of the father, than the father upon account of the son; the servant for the master, than the master for the servant; the subject for the prince, than the prince for the subject." "In short," concludes Hume as if he were Cicero explaining the rhetorical topoi, "our passions, like other objects, descend with greater facility than they ascend" (221–222). This principle applies equally in the case of those two "pure emotions in the soul" that are primarily self-referential—pride and humility—and in the case of mixed emotions such as love and hate that are primarily exo-referential (237). In its radical form, the argument goes like this: no rank, no passion; no passion, no pride; no pride, no self. But is this really Hume? Anyone familiar with his famous work on personal identity should already suspect that it is.

"There are some philosophers," begins the chapter, "who imagine we are every moment intimately conscious of what we call our SELF; that we feel its existence and its continuance in existence; and are certain, beyond the evidence of the demonstration, both of its perfect identity and simplicity. The strongest sensation, the most violent passion, say they, instead of distracting us from this view, only fix it the more intensely, and make us consider the influence on *self* either by their pain or pleasure." But in holding this belief, philosophers such as Descartes and Nicolas de Malebranche are mistaken. "Unluckily all these positive assertions are contrary to that very experience, which is pleaded for them, nor have we any idea of *self*, after the manner it is here explain'd" (164). Perceptions that compose what we call "experience" and seem to refer back to a coherent self are, in fact, explains Hume, simply "a bundle or collection of different perceptions, which succeed each other with an inconceivable rapidity, and are in perpetual flux and movement" (165). But as mundane creatures lacking the infinite forms of thought (omniscience) that would allow us to translate this infinite diversity of experience into action (omnipotence), we feign some "new and unintelligible principle" that connects the objects of thought together and prevents their interruption or variation. "Thus we feign the continu'd existence of the perceptions of our senses, to remove the interruption; and run into the notion of a *soul*, and *self*, and *substance*, to disguise the variation" (166).[3] Although all these "nice and subtle questions concerning personal identity" can never possibly be decided and are to be regarded rather as "grammatical" difficulties (171), Hume himself cannot write without one of his own necessary fictions: "I," admits Hume in the very grammar of his sentence, "cannot compare the soul more properly to any thing than to a republic or commonwealth" (170). As I will show later, this comparison is particularly apt for the sort of fiction, or rhetorical act on a grand scale, that Hume announces in his best-known work *Enquiry concerning Human Understanding*.

Here I will pause in order to weigh the significance of this turn in Hume's argument typically overlooked by analytic philosophers such as Barry Stroud and underestimated even by outstanding scholars of English literature, such as Adela Pinch and Terry Eagleton, who are interested for obvious poststructuralist reasons in Hume's fiction of the self. More than a mere dispute of words (*Treatise*, 166), more than a simple error of thought that could be debunked by way of a philosophical argument (even Hume's), these fictions of the self are built equally into the grammar of everyday life and into the finest arts. Without these fictions performed in their public moment as an eloquent speech that "moves" its audience or in the "force and vivacity" of the poet or storyteller, self would lack the suture that holds it together and prevents madness (84). The most radical implications

3. In Hume's "Dialogues concerning Natural Religion," the character Demea describes men as "finite, weak, and blind creatures." In *Principal Writings on Religion, including Dialogues concerning Natural History and The Natural History of Religion*, ed. J. C. A. Gaskin (Oxford: Oxford University Press, 1998), 43.

of this argument do seem foreclosed: though poetry might conjure a certain vivacity, admits Hume, "how great soever the pitch may be, to which this vivacity rises, 'tis evident, that in poetry it never has the same *feeling* with that which arises in the mind, when we reason." "The mind can easily distinguish betwixt the one and the other," Hume continues, "and whatever emotion the poetical enthusiasm may give to the spirits, 'tis still the mere phantom of belief or perswasion" (84–85). In short, the experience of fancy and reality differ; no doubt, seeing *Oedipus Rex* feels different from being Oedipus Rex.

But remember, reason is eventually reduced to a calm passion (280), rendered "perfectly inert" (294), and then finally deflated altogether by Hume's famous injunction: "Reason is, and ought only to be the slave of the passions, and can never pretend to any other office than to serve and obey them" (266). Moreover, reality itself is not given, but rather is a matter of *persuasion*. Reality, in other words, is ultimately a function of rhetoric as the art of persuasion—which is not to say that all rhetoric is equally persuasive, equally affecting, equal in terms of its power to evoke reality. Some poems, some political speeches, some scientific theories, and some sayings will evoke more powerfully worlds we have experienced in the past and might hope to experience in the future, some less powerfully. Or in Hume's language, certain forms of eloquence will infuse passions into the mind by representing objects in their "strongest and most lively colours," others will not (273). Which gets us back to the soul as a republic or commonwealth.

Evidently, for Hume, what we see in this comparison is eloquence that persuades not by fantastic appeal but rather by way of a "proper" simile that evokes reality. It is not one fiction among others but rather *the* fiction of the soul that is supposed to subordinate all others by way of its vivacity and explanatory power. Hume asserts,

> I cannot compare the soul more properly to any thing than to a republic or commonwealth in which the several members are united

by the reciprocal ties of government and subordination, and give rise
to other persons, who propagate the same republic in the incessant
changes of its parts. And as the same individual republic may not only
change its members, but also its laws and constitution; in like manner
the same person may vary his character and disposition, as well as his
impressions and ideas, without losing his identity. Whatever changes
he endures, his several parts are still connected by the relation of
causation. And in this view our identity with regard to the passions
serves to corroborate that with regard to the imagination, by the
making our distant perceptions influence each other, and by giving
us our present concern for our past or future pains or pleasures. (170)

Personal identity, for instance, must be assumed in order to make
sense of the pain "I" avoid by forswearing public ambition or even
love. But in this very act of self-constitution, the soul is revealed
in its basic vulnerability.

Hume's Pride

"'Tis evident," observes Hume in his famous discussion of the
two key passions, "that pride and humility, tho' directly contrary,
have yet the same OBJECT. This object is self, or that succession
of related ideas and impressions, of which we have an intimate
memory and consciousness" (182). That is to say, the passions of
pride and humility constitute the self—and I will discuss how this
works below—rather than the other way around, where the self is
assumed and the passions are a form of expression. What are some
of the causes of pride and humility? According to Hume, a man
may be proud of mental qualities such as imagination, judgment,
memory, disposition, wit, good sense, learning, courage, justice,
or integrity; physical qualities such as beauty, strength, agility,
good mien, address in dancing, riding, fencing, dexterity in any
manual business or manufacture; or he might be proud of those
objects that are "in the least ally'd or related," such as country,
family, children, relations, riches, houses, gardens, horses, dogs,
or clothes (183). And lest you think this is a relic of the eighteenth-
century bourgeoisie, here is something just as whimsical 150 years

later in that monument of scientific psychology, William James's *The Principles of Psychology* (1890): "*In its widest possible sense . . . a man's Self is the sum total of all that he* CAN *call his*, not only his body and his psychic powers, but his clothes and his house, his wife and children, his ancestors and friends, his reputation and works, his lands and horses, and yacht and bank-account."[4] Something crucial is thereby revealed as Hume, or James for that matter, casts about for causes: since the field of things that cause pride and humility is deeply contoured, the possible formations of self will be shaped accordingly. What exactly, we should wonder, are the contours and by what power are they produced? It turns out that the field of things that cause pride and humility is contoured primarily by principles of *property*, and the sort of selves produced as a result conform to the prejudices built therein.

Thus, neither the passions nor their causes are a matter of mere caprice. Quite the contrary, as Hume clarifies in the *Treatise* and reiterates in the later "Abstract," where he insists that "all our passions are a kind of natural instinct, derived from nothing but the original constitution of the human mind."[5] Pragmatics dictate for Hume that we must assume the passionately constituted self in order to make sense. What we would call comparative anthropology suggests to Hume that "in all nations and ages, the same objects still give rise to pride and humility," such as power, riches, beauty, and personal merit (184). Significantly, however, in the complex analysis of the passions that follows, Hume rejects naturalizing arguments in building the case for intervention in human affairs. Not only is the word *nature* deemed hopelessly ambiguous (304), but passions vary, admittedly, by "very inconsiderable principles" brought to light only by custom and practice. In fact, Hume muses, "if a person full-grown, and of the same nature with ourselves, were on a sudden transported into our world, he wou'd be very much embarrass'd with every object, and not readily find what degree of love or hatred, pride

---

4. William James, *The Principles of Psychology* (New York: Holt, 1890), 291.
5. Hume, *Treatise of Human Nature*, 408.

or humility, or any other passion he ought to attribute to it" (192). One's very being depends upon one's station, and one's station is determined in a social network that has a history. In a sense, we get Marx *avant la lettre*:

> The skin, pores, muscles, and nerves of a day-labourer are different from those of a man of quality: So are his sentiments, actions and manners. The different stations of life influence the whole fabric, external and internal.... Government makes a distinction of property, and establishes the different ranks of man. This produces industry, traffic, manufacturers, law-suits, war, leagues, alliances, voyages, travels, cities, fleets, and all those other actions and objects, which cause such diversity, and the same time maintain such an uniformity in human life. (259)

One cannot assume even the nature of the body, in other words, because in its very material the body is determined quite literally by the politics of social difference. The pores and muscles and emotions of a day-laborer are different from those of a man of quality not because the man of quality is naturally superior, as an earlier generation of Tory satirists such as Alexander Pope and Jonathan Swift might assume, but because *government* makes a distinction of property and establishes the different ranks of men. Human scientist that he is, Hume wants to intervene in human affairs systematically, which means that he must focus his new moral science upon this elusive domain between original nature and human caprice composed of custom, habit, art, and institution—the domain of second nature, where culture and history make all the difference. His analysis is startling.[6]

6. Hume's strategy in this regard is consistent over the course of his life as a man of letters: acknowledge the natural and universal in human nature and then discuss only the unnatural and historical. Here is how he explains variation in religious sentiment in *The Natural History of Religion*: "It would appear, therefore, that this preconception springs not from an original instinct or primary impression of nature, such as gives rise to self-love, affection between the sexes, love of progeny, gratitude, resentment; since every instinct of this kind has been found absolutely universal in all nations and ages." However, "the first religious principles," observes Hume, "must be secondary" (134). Of

After explaining how the association of ideas (and not natural necessity) renders external objects the source of either pride or humility, Hume provides a chilling and very personal example of how the association of ideas works in practice.[7] Those who boast of the antiquity of their families, Hume observes, take special pride when many generations have been uninterrupted proprietors of the same portion of land. "'Tis an additional subject of vanity," continues Hume, when they can boast that these possessions "have been transmitted thro' a descent compos'd entirely of males, and that the honours and fortune have never past thro' any female." It is worth quoting at some length in order to see how Hume works to contain the radical implications of his analysis.

> 'Tis evident that when anyone boasts of the antiquity of his family, the subjects of his vanity are not merely the extent of time and number of ancestors, but also their riches and credit, which are suppos'd to reflect a lustre on himself on account of his relation to them. He first considers these objects; is affected by them in agreeable manner; and then returning back to himself, thro' the relation of parent and child, is elevated with the passion of pride, by means of the double relation of impressions and ideas. Since therefore the passion depends upon these relations, whatever strengthens any of the relations must also encrease the passion, and whatever weakens the relations must diminish the passion. Now 'tis certain the identity of the possession strengthens the relation of ideas arising from blood and kindred, and conveys the fancy with greater facility from one generation to another, from the remotest ancestors to their posterity, who are both their heirs and their descendants. . . . The case is the same with the transmission of the honours and fortune thro' a succession of

course, only these secondary principles are of interest to Hume for the remainder of his discourse.

7. Here is an opening paragraph of Hume's "My Own Life": "I was born the 26th of April 1711, old style, at Edinburgh. I was of a good family, both by father and mother: my father's family is a branch of the Earl of Home's, or Hume's; and my ancestors had been proprietors of the estate, which my brother possesses, for several generations. My mother was daughter of Sir David Falconer, President of the College of Justice: the title of Lord Halkerton came by succession to her brother." In *Principal Writings on Religion.*

males without their passing thro' any female. 'Tis a quality of human nature . . . that the imagination naturally turns to whatever is important and considerable; and where two objects are presented to it, a small and a great one, usually leaves the former, and dwells entirely upon the latter. As in the society of marriage, the male sex has the advantage above the female, the husband first engages our attention; and whether we consider him directly, or reach him by passing thro' related objects, the thought both rests upon him with greater satisfaction, and arrives at him with greater facility than his consort. 'Tis easy to see, that this property must strengthen the child's relation to the father, and weaken that to the mother. . . . This is the reason why children commonly bear their father's name, and are esteem'd to be of nobler or baser birth, according to *his* family. And tho' the mother shou'd be possest of a superior spirit and genius to the father, as often happens, the *general rule* prevails. (201)

In this one passage the radical strains of Humean psychology come together in a fashion that challenges both the way in which we understand possible versions of psyche in the mid-eighteenth-century culture of sensibility and the way in which we late moderns isolate psyche from politics. In this passage we see, as Gilles Deleuze might summarize, the ingenious fashion in which Hume substitutes a psychology of the mind with a psychology of the mind's *affections*.[8] And in doing so, I would add, Hume is less out of step with his time than twentieth-century historians of psychology would have us believe. But more on this in the next section; let us now take a closer look at the crucial passage above.

Though it may be "a quality of human nature" that the imagination turns to whatever is important and considerable, it is clear in this passage that principles of nature have no direct impact on the self so produced. For in this case, the pride of property constitutive of self derives not from any natural principle that dictates how ideas must be associated, nor from some sort of natural superiority of males over females. Indeed, Hume is at pains

8. Gilles Deleuze, *Empiricism and Subjectivity: An Essay on Hume's Theory of Human Nature*, trans. Constantin V. Boundas (New York: Columbia University Press, 1991), 21.

to point out that any particular mother might be superior to her husband in most qualities, but the pride of unbroken patrilineal inheritance will prevail nonetheless. Even the bond between mother and child that we frantically naturalize seems inoperative for Hume, too weak to survive even a mother's second marriage, if it ever existed at all. In the case of a second marriage, the mother's regard is disbursed through the ties of interest and duty that bind her to another family and prevent that "return of the fancy" which is necessary to support the union of mother and child. In contrast, the second marriage of the father does *not* threaten the parental bond, because imagination still projects the father as the head of that family (230–31). What makes the difference in these cases is not nature, but a stable relation, or *institution*: what Hume refers to as the "society of marriage" in which the male sex has both legal and customary advantage over the female. Where the institution is absent, or differently configured, or even differently imagined (as it will be in *David Simple*), then the sort of selves produced will be different as well.

The self is constituted in pride by way of a double gesture whereby the thing—whether object or quality—is simultaneously given social currency as a thing of value and removed from circulation in the phantom form of stable property. My good sense, my good mien, my children, my horses. Thus, personal identity in Hume's scheme is in certain respects analogous to capital in Marx, where stability depends, paradoxically, upon constant mobility and the phantom of absolute value that naturalizes relations of power while rendering them abstract in the form of money. Like Marx in the *Grundrisse*, Hume makes it clear in this example that the naturalized value of fixed capital (property) is in effect a function of cultural capital (patriarchy) circulated not in the deceptively hard currency of cash, but rather in the deceptively soft currency of discourse. "Our reputation, our character, our name are considerations of vast weight and importance," notes Hume elsewhere, "and even the other causes of pride; virtue, beauty and riches; have little influence, when not seconded by the opinions and sentiments of others" (206). Or alternatively, "Every thing in this world is judg'd of by comparison," and therefore the pleasure one might take in the feeling of pride comes not from the sentiment itself, housed somewhere in one's nature, but from a *"communication* of sentiments" (210, my italics). Thus, a person treats strangers with different degrees of respect as he or she is informed of their different fortunes and conditions (234). And when a person once pleased by favorable comparison to his or her inferiors loses ground, "what shou'd only have been a decrease of pleasure," observes Hume, "becomes a real pain" (243). Seemingly immediate feelings of pleasure and pain are, in fact, constituted *between* people who stand in a particular relation to one another; they do not originate "in" one's brain or biology. As the cited example of Hume's favorite son demonstrates in the harshest terms, passions are ultimately a function of discourse in all of its institutional weight. Regardless of the stories that might be told of the mother's particular eminence, a son's self-constituting pride nevertheless depends upon the mother's erasure in the legally sanctioned narrative that gives value to the father's name.

Now tying two threads of my discussion together, it is safe to say that one of Hume's psychic regimes of "government and subordination" is patriarchy. And in light of Hume's appropriation by Anglo-American philosophy, as well as our general inability to consider the politics of emotion, this conclusion is doubly significant. It is terribly misleading, for instance, when Terence Penelhum concludes in his essay on "Hume's Moral Psychology" that Hume's story about the self as social construction "is one we have heard since from Freud, Marx, and the existentialist, always with the ideological accretions wholly foreign to Hume's naturalism."[9] This apolitical reading of Hume could not be further from the truth, in multiple ways.

Contrary to optimistic philosophers of the Scottish Enlightenment such as Hutcheson and Smith, who seem to anchor social passions in a moral sense equally shared by all, Hume

9. Terence Penelhum, "Hume's Moral Psychology," in *The Cambridge Companion to Hume*, ed. David Fate Norton (Cambridge: Cambridge University Press, 1993), 143.

insists that the constitutive power of emotion derives from their *unequal* distribution: "there is no such passion in human minds, as the love of mankind, merely as such, independent of personal qualities" (309). The problem, as Gilles Deleuze noted with extraordinary acumen in his 1953 commentary, is not some natural egoism that dictates self-interest at the expense of society, but rather the contradiction and violence that arises out of "a plurality of partialities." Society, in fact, finds its *obstacle* in sympathies, as Deleuze puts it, because sympathies are always subject to historically circumscribed habits of association (38–39). Sympathy, for Hume, is less a matter of inborn humanity than relative proximity: sentiments are communicated by way of perceived contiguity—who is in and who is out. More like Aristotle in the *Rhetoric* and Thomas Hobbes, Hume outlines in the *Treatise* a "political economy" wherein passions are (1) constituted as differences in power, and (2) conditioned not by their excess, but by their scarcity. As Aristotle's treatment of the master/slave relationship and Hobbes's treatment of vainglory demonstrated in chapter 1, it matters not only where passions are invested, but also where they are denied. The positive function of passions depends upon an economy of scarcity characterized by carefully cultivated apathy. That is to say, it makes a difference not only what sort of passions are distributed to whom, but also how they are hoarded and monopolized and how their systematic denial helps produce selves of a certain sort. In the end, we should be able to account both for those who are full of pride, like Hume's favorite son, and those who are marginalized precisely by their exclusion from passions such as pride, anger, and pity.

Commentators have noted that Hume's discussion of pride and humility says a lot about pride but only a little about humility.[10] There is good reason for this imbalance. Humility poses a basic problem in Hume's scheme that points to a fundamental tension in the culture of sensibility writ large, as I will show in graphic terms when I compare Hume's sensibility to Sarah

10. Pinch, *Strange Fits of Passion* (see introduction, n. 6).

Fielding's. It would seem simple enough: "All agreeable objects, related to ourselves, by an association of ideas and impressions, produce pride, and disagreeable ones, humility" (190). And though directly contrary, both passions are supposed to have the same object: namely, the self, or "that succession of related ideas and impressions of which we have an intimate memory and consciousness" (182). The sensation of humility is uneasy, as that of pride is agreeable. "Accordingly we find," writes Hume, "that a beautiful house, belonging to ourselves, produces pride; and that the same house, still belonging to ourselves, produces humility, when by any accident its beauty is chang'd into deformity, and thereby the sensation of pleasure, which corresponded to pride, is transform'd into pain, which is related to humility" (189).

But there is a problem. What if you don't have a house? Or any of those other objects that are potential sources of pride, such as country, family, children, relations, riches, gardens, horses, dogs, or fine clothes? And what follows from Hume's proprietary notion of having something? As discussed earlier, the laws and customs of patrilineal inheritance dictate that the mother never really "has" even her child, strictly speaking, let alone objects with more distant association. Doesn't Hume's association of ideas and impressions that produce the humble self seem to depend upon the prideful self as the theoretical starting point, an original foil for good things gone bad? Is there really a place in Hume's scheme for a self more experienced with humility? These are crucial questions, considering that elsewhere Hume makes it perfectly clear how custom systematically subordinates the poor, the landless, the powerless, children, Native Americans, and women.[11] At the very least, the humble self is a kind of negative, or inverted, self who experiences the world as a continual flux of disagreeable feelings, threatening people, and lost objects—something like the melancholic whose ego is famously described by Freud as "a precipitate of abandoned object-cathexes."

11. Anne Jaap Jacobson, ed., *Feminist Interpretations of David Hume* (University Park: Pennsylvania State University Press, 2000).

In fact, Hume can help us do what Judith Butler urges in *The Psychic Life of Power*: to think the theory of power together with a theory of the psyche. Like Hume's humble woman whose very sense of self is already constituted by the social narratives and institutions that subordinate her, Butler's melancholic has already withdrawn into the psyche "a configuration of the social world." The ego thus becomes a "polity," as Butler puts it (following Freud), and conscience one of its "major institutions" (*Ichinstitutionen*) precisely because psychic life withdraws a world into itself in an effort to annul the losses that world demands (178, 181). For Butler, in other words, the melancholic is constituted not by some personal inability to cope with a loss, but rather by a prohibition (such as heteronormativity) instituted at the level of culture. And psyche does not precede culture, but rather is produced in the prohibitive turn (or "trope") that variously distinguishes interior from exterior life: "I am this, not that." I have already shown how Hume similarly rejects the false problems of egoism when he compares the soul to a republic in which the several members are united by the reciprocal ties of government and subordination. Like Butler, Hume asks us to consider also how in one particular regime, patriarchy, the prideful souls of privileged men are differently bound to objects (by tropes of metaphor and metonymy) than are the humble souls of women and other subordinates. Both Butler and Hume are deeply interested in challenging the notion of autonomous will and psychological universalism, asking instead what certain kinds of losses are compelled by a set of culturally prevalent prohibitions, and what culturally prevalent forms of psyche result (139). Finally, both ask to what extent masculinity and femininity are formed through differently configured object relations (166).

The problem Butler's psychoanalytic model raises for my interpretation of Hume and, conversely, the problem Hume raises for Butler is the following: what is the precise history of the humble soul's object relations, and how is the psyche thereby produced *different* from that of the melancholic? Though they might be structured in similar ways, the humble and the melancholic are not the same sort of people. This means that their political diagnosis and therapy, so to speak, will differ as well. As if to underscore this point, Hume is careful not to contrast pride with melancholy, which is a word and a disposition familiar enough to the self-described melancholic, who uses the word hundreds of times in his essays and letters.[12] In what remains of this chapter, I wager that closer attention to the relationship between gender, object, and humility (Christian or otherwise) will allow us to implicate politics in the psyche, and do so, moreover, in a manner different from those theorists such as Juliana Schiesari, Carla Mazzio, and Judith Butler, who have recently established melancholy as the pivotal political passion.[13]

In Hume's scheme, the law does weaken the child's relation to the mother, which implies, of course, that there was an object relation to be lost in the first place. But we should seriously consider whether, strictly speaking, Hume's humble self is in fact no self at all, the loss no loss at all. This would help explain how, for instance, after a highly innovative treatment of the passions that includes reversing the long-standing Christian model which pegs pride as the vice and humility as the virtue, Hume can conclude in the most traditional vein that the essential female virtues are modesty and chastity (364). More than some distracted reversion to traditional values, this is a key moment in the *Treatise*'s third and final book, "Of Morals," because it demonstrates in practical terms how culture and psyche are composed asymmetrically around the transfer term *stability*. Unlike the apparent inwardness of melancholia, humility and its accompanying virtues, such as modesty and chastity, are explicitly characterized by their instrumentality in producing certain *other* stable selves. Thus, I might

12. G. J. Barker-Benfield, *The Culture of Sensibility: Sex and Society in Eighteenth-Century Britain* (Chicago: University of Chicago Press, 1992), 27.

13. Juliana Schiesari, *The Gendering of Melancholia: Feminism, Psychoanalysis, and the Symbolics of Loss in Renaissance Literature* (Ithaca, NY: Cornell University Press, 1992); Carla Mazzio, "The Melancholy of Print: *Love's Labour's Lost*," in *Historicism, Psychoanalysis, and Early Modern Culture*, ed. Carla Mazzio and Douglas Trevor (New York: Routledge, 2000).

add, they provide as well a unique site for destabilizing the social order.

Significantly, the structure of book three is idiosyncratic. So idiosyncratic, in fact, that it is radically revised in Hume's later *An Enquiry concerning the Principles of Morals*, where the term *property* does not even appear in the original index. As opposed to the system of ethics from Aristotle and Hugo Grotius to Ralph Cudworth and Samuel Clarke that would treat property as a secondary issue and structure the treatise accordingly, Hume makes property a first principle in the *Treatise* and addresses the topic almost immediately. Ethics is not applied, among other places, to issues of property (for example, justice demands its appropriate distribution); property actually makes ethics possible. We should already suspect why this is so. As opposed to those myriad philosophers who derive moral principles from reason, God-given or natural, Hume derives moral principles from passion. To have a sense of virtue, for Hume, is nothing but "to feel a satisfaction of a particular kind" (303); to have a sense of duty is to follow the "course of our passions" (311). But remember that passions, exemplified by the primary passion of pride, are in turn a function of property defined in sociohistorical terms—including occupation, prescription, accession, and succession—that Hume is compelled to discuss in footnoted detail *before* justice is even addressed (322–30). No property, in other words, no ethics. And it matters the precise historical forms that property takes.

In eighteenth-century England, as Eileen Spring and Susan Staves have persuasively argued, that form is in fact patriarchal, and increasingly so. As opposed to Lawrence Stone and others who have argued that the progressive substitution of contract logic for common law ultimately reflected the improving status of women in eighteenth-century English culture, Spring and Staves have built a compelling case that precisely the opposite is true. In fact, apparent "rights" to either real or personal property that an aristocratic woman might have enjoyed under common law—such as use-rights of dower or the inheritance of an heiress-at-law—were regularly circumvented in eighteenth-century English legal practice and replaced with more flexible procedures such as strict marriage settlements and final testaments that might better maintain a continuous line of inheritance from one male family member to another, even if that meant skipping a generation or preferring a collateral male such as an uncle or nephew to a direct heiress. Particularly revealing for Spring and immediately relevant to my discussion of Hume is the heiress in gentry and aristocratic families who, with the strict marriage settlements of the eighteenth century, "reached her nadir." "She was not to succeed except as a last resort," Spring summarizes, "inheritance would not be traced through her except as a last resort; and her portion, calculated before birth, was calculated at a time when the interests of the patriline were uppermost." In short, Spring concludes, English landowners had moved by the mid-eighteenth century from lineal to patrilineal principles,[14] while among the middle classes patriarchy had been reinforced with new testamentary freedom that could be, and was, used to circumvent the common-law rights of widows (64). If for Hume pride is a function of property defined in sociohistorical terms, then it was apparently in short supply among women when we consider the actual status of women in eighteenth-century England.

Critical legal studies thus suggest that Hume's philosophical interest in the passions of patriarchy coincides with broader social interests discernible in the historical record. The work of Spring and Staves can help us see how, in the Age of Sensibility, masculine pride-in-property trumped universal sympathy, while the passionate ingratitudes of misogyny trumped universal justice. In turn, Hume's theory that masculine pride depends upon feminine humility can help us understand the ideological context for actual court cases well into the nineteenth century. Take for instance the decision by Lord Chancellor Brougham in the famous case of *Howard v. Digby* (1834), where the issue turned on whether so-called pin money, or pocket money, was simply

14. Eileen Spring, *Law, Land, and Family: Aristocratic Inheritance in England, 1300 to 1800* (Chapel Hill: University of North Carolina Press, 1993), 18–19.

supposed to be for a wife's maintenance or whether it was supposed to be for expenses more "fanciful and luxurious." As Susan Staves reports, the Whig Chancellor concluded in his opinion that the money is not meant to secure the woman in perpetuity by providing an inalienable capital fund, nor that it should bolster a woman's pride by securing personal property such as fine dress and jewelry. On the contrary, Chancellor Brougham opines, pin money is ultimately meant "to dress the wife so as to keep up the dignity of the *husband*."[15] This sounds absurd to our ears and was extraordinarily ideological even for its own time. The sentiment is clear, however, and, as an appeal to the lords, it did carry the day. In an age challenged by newly mobile forms of property and population, the stability of personality and society so important to Hume and his contemporaries demanded a particular kind of asymmetry that, although unsystematic in its means, systematically disadvantaged women in the end. Moreover, this disadvantage extended much beyond the rights to one's person or to either real or personal property and well into that inherently unstable domain of social discourse and imagination, where proprietary habits are first cultivated and finally maintained. In fact, the more unstable the form of property, Hume suggests, the more important is a new science of morals that might reassert some degree of stability.

After pointing out in the *Treatise* that mental and physical qualities cannot be appropriated and therefore have minimal ethical significance, Hume turns his attention once again to the third, most fragile and most interesting species of goods that serve as the material alibi around which civil society emerges: possessions acquired by industry and good fortune. Only this last sort of possession is both scarce and exposed to violent appropriation. "As the improvement, therefore, of these goods is the chief advantage of society," Hume observes, "so the *instability* of their possession,

15. Susan Staves, *Married Women's Separate Property in England, 1660–1833* (Cambridge, MA: Harvard University Press, 1990), 155–56; see also John Brewer and Susan Staves, eds., *Early Modern Conceptions of Property* (London: Routledge, 1995).

along with their *scarcity*, is the chief impediment" (313). This fact dictates the desirable shape of civil society and the sort of souls it is meant to inhabit. It means, among other things, that the shape of civil society will be derived not from nature but from *artifice*. For when people observe that the principal disturbance in society arises from those goods called "external," and from their "looseness and easy transition from one person to another," they must seek a remedy that puts these goods on the same footing with relatively constant advantages of mind and body. There is no other way to do this, concludes Hume, "than by a convention enter'd into by all the members of the society to bestow stability on the possession of those external goods, and leave every one in the peaceable enjoyment of what he may acquire by his fortune and industry" (314). Hence the detailed discussion in succeeding sections "Of the rules which determine property," "Of the transference of property by consent," and so forth. In the end, it is more than civil society that is threatened when external goods do not stay put, and more than what J. G. A. Pocock calls "political personality," caught between the older agrarian model of ownership and the newer commercial model.[16] The very sense of self is threatened at its political moorings. This is why Hume's often radical revision of ethics can swerve back to a conservative conclusion that ideally *"every one continue to enjoy what he is at present possess'd of "* (323). No instability of property, no instability of self, which is Hume's ultimate concern when it comes to a science of morality.

But what if "one" does not have a sense of self to lose in the first place, which seems to be the case for those who either do not have external goods or have them only by proxy—for instance, married women dispossessed of both separate property and even a control over their own bodies proportional to that enjoyed by men? When Hume justifies another set of traditional duties,

16. J. G. A. Pocock, *Virtue, Commerce, and History: Essays on Political Thought and History, Chiefly in the Eighteenth Century* (Cambridge: Cambridge University Press, 1985), 70–71.

namely, "the *modesty* and *chastity* which belong to the fair sex" (364), the radical asymmetry of patriarchy becomes clear, and with it the diversity of selves thereby produced. The story is familiar enough. If men are to share with women the burdens of rearing children, they must believe that the children are their own and that "their natural instinct is not directed to a wrong object, when they give a loose to love and tenderness" (364). But since the principle of generation, as Hume puts it, goes from the man to the woman, an error is possible only in the man's case. From this trivial anatomical observation, Hume concludes, is derived "that vast difference betwixt the education and duties of the two sexes." In this case, legal injunction seems to Hume insufficient, because infidelity is difficult to prove in court. Thus, there seems to be nothing to restrain women but the punishment of "bad fame or reputation": shame imposed for infidelity—or even those expressions, postures, and liberties *associated* with infidelity—and proportional praise for chastity, or those expressions, postures, and liberties associated with chastity. In this way, the virtues of modesty and chastity take on broad cultural significance beyond the married couple in childbearing years and extend to the domain of language and imagination (364–66). But the more attenuated the connection between a woman's virtue and her best interest, the more vulnerable her moral character. Language and imagination, after all, might be used to subvert the very system of gender they ought to support.

The stability of the self that men enjoy in a regime of patriarchy depends directly upon the woman's role as *vehicle*. What makes Hume's scheme extraordinary is that he theorizes in exquisite detail the interanimation of politics and psyche and thus unwittingly reveals how any particular regime of the soul might be dismantled, including the regime of patriarchy that he explicitly endorses. Even for Hume, the dismantling of patriarchy would mean more than justice fairly redistributed between men and women. It would mean, instead, a radical refashioning of the institutions of language, passion, and imagination that constitute the gendered psyche in the first place, a progressive rhetoric, in other words, that would build community in a new way by extending the range of objects about which a woman could legitimately feel a sense of pride.

To summarize the problem in psychoanalytic terms: where the melancholic are unable to mourn lost objects, the humble are unable to extend a sense of ownership. And though these two sorts of souls are similarly determined by what they lack, their difference is material when it comes to articulating a scientific response, as Hume would do. Whereas the problem of melancholia suggests to Judith Butler that one mobilize anger turned inward, the problem of humility suggests that one mobilize the expansive imagination. This turns out to be precisely the function of an eloquent politician, according to Hume: "the utmost politicians can perform, is, to extend the natural sentiments beyond their original bounds" and thereby extend the range of objects over which the political subject can feel a sense of ownership (321).[17] Psychology, in short, as a therapeutic rhetoric of the body politic.

Human Science as Rhetoric

The paradox of masculine pride that threatens Hume's system is the same paradox that threatens the new man of the Enlightenment generally: his pride, and thus his very agency in the expanding sphere of politics and commerce, depends upon a basic vulnerability to institutions of language and association not of his own making. His expanding agency, in short, depends upon the feminine passivity characteristic of a polite and well-disciplined society. In substituting a psychology of the mind with a psychology of the mind's affections, moreover, Hume's theory invites a radical critique of the social customs and schemes of subordination that affect the mind, including the very customs and schemes that ideally constitute the new subject of the human sciences as

17. In performing this function, the politician distinguishes himself from the vast majority of preachers, whose utmost task seems to Hume the inculcation of terror. See Hume, *Principal Writings on Religion*, 128, 140.

a virile agent in the public sphere. As already mentioned, this critique stops short of its revolutionary implications by arguing consistently for the stability of the status quo and thus for the stability of privileged, masculine selves at the expense of women and other subordinates. But Hume is equally consistent in presenting his new human science as a radical intervention in human affairs, rather than a descriptive science of the mind. Hume's famous introduction to *An Enquiry concerning Human Understanding* and his essays on the function of the arts and sciences make this abundantly clear. When human science functions as a kind of therapeutic rhetoric, as it does for Hume, the new man of the Enlightenment is revealed in his basic passivity. To put this another way, the new man is feminized in his new virtue, and the weakness of patriarchy is thereby tested at its very foundation.

In Anglo-American circles, it is typical, but wildly misleading, to characterize Hume's project primarily as a sober (i.e., masculine) and doggedly empirical project that anticipates twentieth-century positivism. In fact, as Hume describes his own project and as he executes it, both its means and its ends are explicitly *rhetorical*; that is to say, Hume's project is purposefully eloquent, passionately interventionist, and unabashedly utopian. "Moral philosophy, or the science of human nature," as Hume famously proclaims in the first sentence of his *Enquiry*, should promote no less than the "entertainment, instruction, and reformation of mankind."[18] Certainly not the end of a sober natural philosophy or natural science, these are precisely the classical humanist ends of rhetoric: *delectare, docere, movere.* Where the abstruse philosopher considers people in the light of a reasonable rather than an active being and endeavors "to form his understanding more than cultivate manners," Hume's moral philosopher "enters more into common life; moulds the heart and affections; and, by touching those principles which actuate man, reforms their conduct, and brings them nearer to the model of perfection which it describes"

---

18. David Hume, *An Enquiry concerning Human Understanding*, ed. Tom L. Beauchamp (Oxford: Oxford University Press, 1999), 87.

(87–88). In other words, Hume's project is designed to soften, even to feminize, manners on a grand scale by exploiting the soft underbelly of reason. It is worth quoting this important opening passage of the *Enquiry* at length. Philosophers of the second species, Hume elaborates,

> paint her [i.e., virtue] in the most amiable colours; borrowing all helps from poetry and eloquence, and treating their subject in an easy and obvious manner, and such as is best fitted to please the imagination, and engage the affections. They select the most striking observations and instances from common life; place opposite characters in a proper contrast; and alluring us into the paths of virtue by the views of glory and happiness, direct our steps in these paths by the soundest precepts and most illustrious examples. They make us *feel* the difference between vice and virtue; they excite and regulate our sentiments; and so they can but bend our hearts to the love of probity and true honour. (87)

The means of human science are rhetorical: the effective moral philosopher should draw from the arts of poetry and eloquence to paint virtue in the most amiable colors, pleasing the imagination with striking observations and illustrious examples. Likewise, the ends are rhetorical: our imagination is pleased [*delectare*] by these views of glory and happiness, our understanding is taught [*docere*] the soundest moral principles, and finally we are moved [*movere*] in our very being—the ultimate goal of human science as a mode of intervention. Like every aspect of Hume's "suasive art,"[19] this effort to move souls invokes the tradition of rhetoric running back to classical antiquity, particularly to the debate regarding the relative virtues of pathos and logos in the science of argumentation. What Hume ultimately does with this tradition is, however, extraordinary.

Supposedly volatile and even blinding, the emotions have always been treated with caution by those who would hail the

---

19. M. A. Box, *The Suasive Art of David Hume* (Princeton, NJ: Princeton University Press, 1990).

virtues of rational discourse aimed at truth.[20] And since Plato, such caution is the symptom of a profoundly divisive political philosophy separating experts from the masses. As Plato suggests via Socrates in the *Gorgias*, a famous diatribe against rhetorical art, the rhetorician might have some luck arguing to the ignorant about something like the causes of health and sickness, but among those who know, the diagnosis of a trained doctor will carry more weight. However, the doctor's authority in this case comes not from his character alone (ethos) or his ability to excite auditors via pathos. Rather, the doctor is more convincing because he is familiar with the technical domain at issue, and, based on this knowledge, he can construct a reasonable verbal depiction that corresponds to the facts in a self-evident manner. Ideally, the doctor's argument is thus transparent and is "convincing" only insofar as it is aimed at equals and reveals the true order of nature. Ultimately, the Platonic scientist persuades his colleagues of nothing, moves them nowhere. Instead, he illuminates the truth by way of a self-negating logos, thus making the foundation upon which he and his colleagues already stand that much more secure. The sophistic rhetorician, on the other hand, "has no need to know the truth about things but merely to discover a technique of persuasion, so as to appear among the ignorant to have more knowledge than the expert" (459c). And as the Roman rhetoricians would later insist, the most powerful persuasive technique entails manipulating the passions of a mass audience.

In typical Roman fashion, Cicero acknowledges that it is important for a person involved in civic affairs to give human emotions voice, but only in order to make proofs exciting to those who might otherwise remain apathetic. As Cicero expresses in *De oratore* through the character of Antonius, intellectual understanding might have a direct line to the truth, but that line will usually remain untapped unless some external motivating force is

---

20. A more detailed discussion can be found in my introduction to Gross and Kemmann, *Heidegger and Rhetoric* (see introduction, n. 15).

applied. Thus, a civic leader must work the emotions of his colleagues and subjects (where Hume's philosopher might "bend our hearts") and employ eloquent speech to do so (Hume's "amiable colours"). In the words of Cicero's Antonius: "that passionate style searches out an arbitrator's emotional side rather than his understanding, and that side can only be reached by diction that is rich, diversified and copious, with animated delivery to match. Thus concise or quiet speakers may inform an arbitrator, but cannot excite him, on which excitement everything depends" (2.52.214). Eloquence is more powerful than a dry appeal to the facts, and thus it can be the only means of persuasion available, even to the well-meaning orator. Quintilian would reluctantly defend eloquence two generations later with the following compromise: "appeals to emotion are necessary if there are no other means for securing the victory of truth, justice and the public interest" (*Institutio oratoria*, 6.1.7).

Obviously, lurking in the Roman defense of eloquence is the fear that emotional appeals present a danger to civil society. Indeed, Cicero asserts through the voice of Catulus that an orator can be trained to manipulate human emotions for his own ends, rather than for the general good. Such cynical sentiments make it plausible to Quintilian that Athenians actually tried to forbid emotional appeals in the legal arena, futile though that might seem. And Quintilian has no doubt that philosophers deemed susceptibility to emotion a vice, thinking it "immoral that the judge should be distracted from the truth by an appeal to his emotions and that it is unbecoming for a good man to make use of vicious procedure to serve his ends" (*Institutio oratoria*, 6.1.7). So logical reason by itself escapes the common person, while a thoughtless appeal to emotion can be subject to abuse. The Roman solution to this dilemma was to add pathos to logos, to join reason and eloquence—and this by sheer fiat. Perhaps the most influential statement to this effect is furnished in the opening pages of *De inventione*, where Cicero admits that, because eloquence without wisdom is blind and wisdom without eloquence is mute, the two should always be conjoined: *ratio atque oratio* (1.1). Logos and pathos must be joined as a pragmatic compromise oriented toward the true and the common good, but this compromise and its orientation are by no means necessary in a philosophical sense: rather, they are a posteriori and contingent upon the arduous training in virtue expected of a Roman citizen.

Superficially this might sound like Hume's moral philosopher who borrows techniques from poetry and eloquence in order to better engage the affections of the common person and thereby draw people into the paths of virtue. But it is not, as we should suspect when we recall Hume's dictum that reason is, and ought only to be, the slave of the passions. Instead of cynically manipulating those superficial beliefs that overlie essential reason, Hume's moral philosopher touches those principles that *actuate* man in the first place, reforming thereby his very being. Hume's training in classical rhetoric has been well documented, particularly his lifelong fascination with Cicero; Hume's exploitation of rhetoric in the presentation of his own philosophy has been treated extensively in two book-length studies, *The Suasive Art of David Hume* and *The Fate of Eloquence in the Age of Hume*.[21] However, this strong claim of Hume's rhetoric has been underestimated, with the consequence that his human science has been underestimated as well. For Hume, the key to human science as a rhetorical art is the cultivation not of reason but of passion, and this means cultivating not only the strong passions that overwhelm people—such as love and hate, anger and joy—but also the passive dispositions that compose people, such as the ability to listen, to feel, to learn, to obey, and to change for the better.

This is why Hume winds up asking a rhetorical question that seems to us out of place in an essay on "The Rise and Progress of the Arts and Sciences" but is typical in the Age of Sensibility: "What better school for manners, than the company of virtuous women; where the mutual endeavour to please must insensibly polish the mind, where the example of the female softness and

---

21. Adam Potkay, *The Fate of Eloquence in the Age of Hume* (Ithaca, NY: Cornell University Press, 1994).

modesty must communicate itself to their admirers, and where the delicacy of that sex puts everyone on his guard, lest they give offense by any breach of decency."[22] And this is why, despite his strong criticism of religious enthusiasm, Hume's proper office of the politician can sound a lot like the proper office of the preacher: that is, to "regulate the heart of men, humanize their conduct, infuse the spirit of temperance, order, and obedience" (122). The irony of Hume's project—from the 1740 *Treatise*, his first significant published work, to his final *Dialogues concerning Natural Religion* almost forty years later in 1779—is that the masculine pride that seems essential to the well-being of society depends upon feminine humility that starts out simply as man's vehicle, but winds up transforming the very sentiments that actuate him. Virtuous women—that "timorous and pious sex" (144)—tame the excesses of pride upon which man's sense of self is built, while introducing in place of vanity a host of feminine virtues that soften him. This irony produces a fundamental tension in Hume's thought and in the texts he produces over the course of his literary career, a tension, I have argued throughout this book, that is fundamental to a form of modernity that simultaneously champions agency in the public sphere while disavowing the passive obedience that makes this agency possible. Compare, for instance, Hume's attack in *The Natural History of Religion* on the "monkish virtues" of mortification, penance, humility, and passive suffering (163) to his essay on "Passive Obedience" and his *History of England*, in which he concludes a discussion of the English Civil War and the tragic execution of King Charles with the observation that "the doctrine of obedience ought alone to be *inculcated*."[23]

Agents in the public sphere get it coming and going. The new sense of agency that comes from a favorable comparison to the

---

22. Hume, "Of the Rise and Progress of the Arts and Sciences," in *Essays, Moral, Political, and Literary*, ed. T. H. Green and T. H. Grose (Aalen: Scientia Verlag, 1992), 194.

23. David Hume, *The History of England* (Indianapolis: Liberty Classics, 1983), 5:544.

gods and marks the modern virtues of "activity, spirit, courage, magnanimity, and love of liberty" endangers a civil society where a favorable comparison to the monarch produces terrible instability.[24] No wonder Hume is unable to describe humility as a positive condition for political subjectivity or some other strong form of the self. Humility, after all, is the negative condition necessary to produce a positive condition of pride. And no wonder Hume personifies humility and other passive dispositions as peculiarly female. Like his contemporaries, from Joseph Addison at the beginning of the Age of Sensibility to Jeremy Bentham at the end, Hume creates an elaborate but ultimately fragile mechanism for disavowing the vulnerability upon which masculine agency depends. In doing so, moreover, Hume represents the basic anxiety of the human scientists populating the eighteenth-century literary and cultural world with their new theories of people: human scientific projects demand a susceptibility to change that implicates everyone, including, ultimately, the human scientist him- or herself.

In its very negativity, humility figures as a crucial fiction of the eighteenth-century self that shapes not only conflicted versions of masculinity and femininity, but also the literature that gives these versions of self a graphic form. Like Hume, however, we have lost the ability to read humble characters and their diffuse narratives as much more than inadequate—the critical reception of Sarah Fielding's *David Simple* is a case in point.[25] My discussion of

24. As Terry Eagleton summarizes this tension in his brief but brilliant analysis of Hume in *The Ideology of the Aesthetic*, "the law is male" (for instance, the property law that institutes patriarchy) but "hegemony is a woman." As Eagleton sees it, Hume is well aware that the laws themselves have no metaphysical sanction, dependent as they are upon the very habits of thought and manner they institute. It is no wonder that Hume's human science is structured as a rhetorical art, designed as it is to treat passions and tropes. Eagleton, *The Ideology of the Aesthetic* (Oxford: Basil Blackwell, 1990), 58.

25. Gary Gaultier, "Henry and Sarah Fielding on Romance and Sensibility," *Novel: A Forum on Fiction* 31, no. 2 (1998): 195–214; Alexander Pettit, "*David Simple* and the Attenuation of 'Phallic Power,'" *Eighteenth-Century Fiction* 11, no. 2 (1999): 169–84; Betty A. Schellenberg, *The Conversational Circle: Rereading the English Novel,*

Hume thus far on the gender of pride and humility should help us break that critical habit. We should now be able to ask not only what is missing from the shallow psyche and meager action of the humble character as he or she compares to the developed character and plot of *Joseph Andrews*, but also how character and plot in a novel such as *David Simple* are complex precipitates of passion. More precisely, in reading Fielding's novel, published just four years after Hume's *Treatise*, we should be able to analyze with greater acuity how patriarchy as a psychic form of government and subordination is imagined in mid-century England and how authors such as Hume and Fielding characterize it with different degrees of resistance.

In her novel *The Adventures of David Simple* (1744) and its sequel *Volume the Last* (1753),[26] Sarah Fielding tells a sophisticated story of humility-in-action that points directly to the paradox of agency vexing someone like Hume and works out in fine detail what might happen if a particular subculture imagined property relations very differently. In doing so, Fielding sketches the limits and possibilities of agency at the critical moment when human science—exemplified by Hume's *Treatise*—struggled to distinguish itself in a world where the passive virtues of Christ still provided a model for imitation. Rather than being just a premodern curiosity that pales in comparison to the novels of her friend and correspondent Samuel Richardson or her brother Henry Fielding, Sarah Fielding's novel is a noteworthy feminist counternarrative of a "modernity-imagined-otherwise" that continues to challenge certain dominant narratives of modernity and, as such, represents the ongoing possibilities of literature as a critical human science.

1740–1775 (Lexington: University Press of Kentucky, 1996), 2. See also Felicity Nussbaum, "Effeminacy and Femininity: Domestic Prose Satire and David Simple," *Eighteenth-Century Fiction* 11, no. 4 (1999): 422–44.

26. Sarah Fielding, *The Adventures of David Simple and Volume the Last*, ed. Peter Sabor (Lexington: University Press of Kentucky, 1998).

The Humility of David Simple

Since Hume and Fielding posit what amounts to inverse fictions of modernity composed in close proximity, it should come as no surprise that their fictions share a number of features, the most significant of which is the assumption that social passions constitute personal identity. To begin with, Fielding expressly positions her "moral romance" much like Hume's "moral philosophy" designed, if you recall, to portray "our identity with regard to the passions" and thereby improve humanity (*Treatise*, 170). Unlike traditional French romances of the seventeenth century by the likes of Madeleine de Scudéry and Honoré d'Urfé that overstimulate the imagination and fill a girl's head with "nothing but love,"[27] Fielding's fiction about a singularly unambitious bachelor who sets off through the world in order to meet a "real friend" is designed to paint a pattern of the passions worthy of imitation. When, toward the beginning of his travels, David visits a circle of women (and a few inconsequential men) eager to prove their taste and wit by discussing literature in the superficial terms of "genius," "invention," "imagery," and "diction," David feels obliged to give his simple opinion about the virtues of literature, and he does so in a manner that one cannot help but read as Fielding's own views about literature and its ends. "The only Way of writing well," insists David to one of his faux friends, Spatter, is "to draw all the Characters from Nature, and to affect the Passions in such a manner, as the *Distresses* of the Good should move Compassion, and that Amiableness of their Actions incite Men to imitate them; and the *Vices* of the Bad stir up Indignation and Rage." This is the "only kind of Writing useful to Mankind," David concludes, "tho' there might be Embellishments, and Flights of Imagination, to amuse and to avert the Reader" (68).

Besides the invocation of now familiar ends of rhetoric—*movere, delectare, docere*—what is noteworthy in this passage is

27. Ibid., 41.

the ambiguity of passions at the same time "drawn from nature" and affected. Affected by whom, first of all? By the author who draws? By the characters drawn? By the men who read the writing and whose compassion is thereby moved? While skillfully complicating both the relationship between nature and art, and between agent and patient, Fielding reminds us in this passage that passions are for her, and for her contemporaries including Hume, much more than irrational feelings expressed by individuals. The sort of language Fielding and Hume use to characterize passion is in fact striking in its similarity. Describing David's future wife, Camilla, for instance, Fielding returns to the traditional Christian hierarchy of virtues overturned by Hume, but in doing so she recalls Hume's radical constructivism that posits no self beyond the social passions that constitute it. Camilla's mind is "totally void of Pride" and fully composed of that relational passion of modesty, of which she is "the most exact Pattern" (220). And where Hume's moral philosopher, if you remember, "moulds the heart and affections; and, by touching those principles which actuate man, reforms their conduct" (87–88), Fielding's David is described as "a Man, actuated by neither Avarice nor Ambition, his Mind moving on no other Axis but that of Love" (245). Love, for Fielding, is by no means a passion that bubbles up mysteriously from the heart and attaches to people simply according to nature. For Fielding, as for Hume, a passion so natural seeming as filial or parental love is composed in a dynamic field of social difference where even the false perception of ingratitude, such as that imposed by the jealous stepmother, Livia, upon Camilla's good-natured father, can precipitate a real decline in parental affection (117–19). The exclusive axis of David's love extends to Camilla not as the object of romantic love untouched by community ethics, but rather as a wife of whom "his Judgment approves" (245). And finally, real happiness is described by Fielding at the end of the novel as a community in which every member performs the part allotted by his or her "*Station in Life*," without begrudging the advantages of one's superiors (237). Ultimately for both Hume and Fielding, there is no other

axis of the mind, no other principle that activates human potential, than passion-as-social-difference. When the activating
principle is relatively unadulterated—as it seems to be for the
thoroughly modest Camilla or thoroughly humble David—the
character appears to us psychologically shallow, especially when
compared to someone like Orguiel, whose character arcs through
a more vexed combination of pride and compassion. But read as
an authorial strategy at odds with what Patricia Meyer Spacks
calls the mid-century plots of "phallic power" and a masculine
agency centered in pride, Fielding's characterizations are much
more compelling.[28]

At every critical turn, Fielding foils the expectations of plot
and character developed in comic romance and still, in many
respects, held today. At the moment David asks for Camilla's
hand in marriage, Fielding's narrative breaks off abruptly so as
to frustrate romantic convention: "I shall not dwell minutely on
this Part of my Hero's Life, as I have too much Regard for my
Readers to make them *third Persons to Lovers*;—and shall only
inform the Curious, that *Camilla*, on the Consideration that
she had already received such strong Proofs of *David*'s sincere
Affection,—thought proper to abate something of the *Ceremonies*
prescribed to Lovers" (230). So not only does Fielding frustrate
the romantic convention that would saturate a marriage proposal
with the pathos of release, she does so by drawing attention to
the particular affective expectations a reader brings to the novel,
the most significant of which is the expectation that he or she
will enjoy witnessing the frustrated phallic hero finally seduce
the object of his desire. As she is wont to do, Fielding chooses
instead to signal the heroic plot points carefully circumvented
and to reinvest the reader's affection in the conventional object
of desire whose pivotal "action" is composed precisely of strategic nonaction: Camilla thinks it proper to "abate the ceremonies
prescribed to lovers." And though the novel ends conventionally

28. Patricia Meyer Spacks, *Desire and Truth: Functions of Plot in Eighteenth-Century
English Novels* (Chicago: University of Chicago Press, 1990).

with a double wedding of David and Camilla, and Valentine and
Cynthia, Fielding refuses to luxuriate in the details, challenging once again the affective investments of the reader: "Perhaps
it may be here expected I should give some Description of the
Persons of my favourite Characters; but as the Writers of Novels
and Romances have already exhausted all the Beauties of Nature
to join their Heroes and Heroines, I shall leave it to my Readers
Imagination to form them just as they liked best: It is their Minds
I have taken most pains to bring them acquainted with, and from
that Acquaintance it will be easy to judge what Scheme of Life
was followed by this whole Company" (236). As opposed to the
phallic protagonist, such as Tom Jones or Mr. B., whose actions
drive the plot from quest to conquest to conjugation,[29] David and
his cohorts are rigorously constructed by Fielding as evacuated
characters that effectively deconstruct the conventional romantic
plot point by point and thereby force the reader to imagine how
affective investments might work differently.

By way of Cynthia's pathetic autobiography about the tribu-
lations of an intelligent girl spitefully refused property by her
father, we see that Fielding's narrative shares major coordinates
with Hume, though the possibilities Fielding realizes within this
patriarchal world are markedly different in the end. Cynthia is
both a founding member of David's "little Society" (237) and
David's first love. His love is born of compassion and admiration
but sacrificed in the name of Cynthia's fidelity; for we learn that
in her youth Cynthia had secretly liked a different young gen-
tleman, Valentine (Camilla's brother), whom she will eventually
marry. Cynthia's story that "amazed" David (93) tells of her cruel
parents and siblings, who upbraid her with being a "wit" more
interested (like Fielding, presumably) in reading Lord Kames
on criticism or the moralist Jean de La Bruyère than finding a
husband. Disregarding her actual character, we learn, Cynthia's
father secures her an offer of marriage and delivers the news to
Cynthia with the following command: "*I expect your Obedience;*

29. Pettit, "*David Simple*," 170.

you know, your Mother always obeyed me, and I will be Master of my own Family." These ridiculous words prompt Cynthia to recall, "I really could hardly forbear laughing in his face" (85). In fact, Cynthia's wit consistently challenges crass economic assumptions of patriarchy. Thus, when her suitor informs her that he and her father "were agreed on a bargain," she replies sarcastically that she did not know her father was "of any Trade or had any Goods to dispose of." But if he had, Cynthia continues, and they could agree on their terms, he should have her consent, because "I never interfered with any Business of my Father's" (86). However, liking her "person" and eager to have a (male) heir to his estate, the suitor tries in vain to recover with an offer of luxurious living. To this Cynthia saucily replies that she has no ambition to be his "upper servant" and reflects upon the similarities between a prostitute and a kept wife who marries a man with an estate over which she has no more command than if she were a "perfect stranger" and whose passion she serves even in her efforts to secure her own modicum of pride. "Some Men, indeed," replies Cynthia, "delight in seeing their Wives finer than their Neighbours, which to some Women, whose whole Thoughts are bent on fine Clothes, may be a Pleasure; but for my part, I should in that case think myself just in the Situation of the Horse who wears *gaudy Trappings* only to gratify his *Master's* Vanity, whilst he himself is not at all considered in it." Cynthia then tells David that her desire to live on the interest of her own little fortune without subjecting herself to the humors of a man she disliked was foiled when her father, in his anger at her impudence, made a will in which he left her nothing (87). Thus, Cynthia winds up serving a Lady who forces her to reckon with the instrumental apathy demanded of any slave: "I was to have no *Passions*, no *Inclinations* of my own, but was to be turned into a piece of Clock-Work, which her Ladyship was to wind up or let down, as she pleased" (91).

For Fielding as for Hume, the very passions, such as pride and humility, that constitute personal identity are inherently political and unevenly distributed. I can therefore organize my inquiry at this point by asking of Fielding the question I first asked of Hume: what exactly are the politics of pride and humility? How do pride and humility map onto available regimes of government and subordination, especially onto the regime of patriarchy and its customary object relations? By way of this comparison, we can better read individual texts not as mere instantiations of antiquated ideologies, but rather as strategic moves shaping the peculiarly modern rhetorical field—still in many respects operative for us—in which people are identified and ultimately situated with regard to one another. When we do, we discover that David as a man of feeling acts out the passive conditions of cultural subjectivity disavowed by the agent of patriarchy.

In Cynthia's story, we see how pride and humility map onto the eighteenth-century English regime of patriarchy and its customary object relations in a pattern of resistance.[30] Recalling for us the critical legal history of Staves and Spring, Cynthia's story provides an imaginary case study of how the apparent "rights" to either real or personal property that the daughter of gentry might have enjoyed under common law could be circumvented in eighteenth-century English legal practice and replaced with more flexible procedures such as the final testament subject to the hateful whims of a father. We see how, in the Age of Sensibility, masculine pride-in-property trumped universal sympathy, while the passionate ingratitudes of misogyny trumped universal justice. In the suitor's vain plea, we also see how emotional investment in patrilineal succession could come at the cost of emotional and financial investment in a wife or daughter. But in telling Cynthia's story, Fielding draws more precisely the melancholy consequences of a particular regime of object relations, a regime counterposed point by point by the "little society" Cynthia eventually joins. Finally, Cynthia's story adds depth to the observation

30. In *Common Ground: Eighteenth-Century English Satiric Fiction and the Poor* (Stanford, CA: Stanford University Press, 1997), Judith Frank explores a related issue in Frances Burney's *Cecelia* (1782), arguing that paternalism requires women as an intermediary to absorb and to shape into shame and grief the impact of reorganized labor practices and the accompanying wound to the laboring poor (158).

that passion is a function of social difference, or more precisely (in Humean terms) that masculine pride depends upon feminine humility, fitting as it does into the same ideological world as the case of *Howard v. Digby*. But as opposed to Hume's defense of the status quo composed from the dominant perspective, Cynthia's story is composed from the self-conscious perspective of a subordinate talking her way out of an oppressive regime and into David's utopian circle, where property relations are conceived very differently.

That difference becomes clear in "a very uncommon Dialogue" between David and a moneylender, Mr. Nichols, to whom David appeals toward the end of *Volume the Last* as his fortunes have taken a drastic turn for the worse. The issue turns on whether a letter David has been sent by Valentine telling of his good fortune might secure a loan.

MR. NICHOLS. "And pray, Sir, please to shew me the Bond, or Note, or what kind of Security you are possessed of, by which, if Mr. *Valentine* should have the Success he mentions, you may legally recover any Monies of him."

DAVID. "I have no Bond, or Note, Sir; *Valentine* is my Brother, my Wife's Brother, and that's the same thing."

NICHOLS. "All's one for that, Sir, as you observe, whether he is your Wife's Brother, or your own; but if you have no Security, no Monies will be forthcoming. A Brother, indeed! I have sent Officers with Executions into many a Man's House, whose Brothers might have prevented it, and even with very inconsiderable Loss to themselves."

DAVID. "If there are any such Wretches, Sir, that's nothing to my *Valentine*. We have always lived as one Family, and considered no separate Property."

Of course these extralegal arrangements mean nothing to the moneylender Nichols, though they pique his interest in the quaint emotional economy of David's happy family. "But, for Curiosity sake," asks Nichols, "pray, Sir, answer me one Question, in this *sharing* and living as one Family, that you talk so much about, has it been most in Mr. *Valentine*'s Power to serve you, or yours to serve him? in short, which has conferred the most Obligations?"

To which David of course replies that the word *obligation* is unheard of in his family, though circumstances had, until the recent reversal of fortune, allowed him the pleasure of being able to serve his brother. Nichols, shaking his head, replies that this obligation owed David is a very bad sign indeed if he wants to secure his debt with Valentine's good will, since the only thing obligation produces is resentment and ingratitude. David despairs, "You don't talk our Language, Sir," to which Nichols responds with a sneer (289–90).

The novel presents Sarah Fielding with a formal problem and a related moral dilemma, which I believe she engages admirably, and in doing so Fielding points to a pivotal paradox of modern subjectivity. The formal problem is that novelistic storytelling is built by convention around male characters who do things in an environment where the tensions of social difference—usually of class, gender, and geography—precipitate emotional crises that only an aggressive protagonist can resolve; think of aristocratic Mr. B. cultivating the virtuous servant girl Pamela after giving up on the prospects of sexual assault. The moral dilemma is that this form of storytelling delights the reader precisely by pitting the active vices of men against the passive virtues of women who suffer their exploits. The result is a diminished moral world where the passive virtues, such as patience, obedience, and humility, inadvertently take on a negative value associated primarily with degraded women or feminized men, neither of whom, despite whatever moral lessons they might teach, hold much promise of entertainment in themselves. Fielding's strategy is to imagine a little society-within-society controlled for differences in class, gender, and geography, and thereby to reformulate for a modern, commercial world what character and plot would look like if composed around the predominant passion of humility, rather than pride. But in doing so, Fielding produces more than a nice thought experiment lacking dramatic tension. In working out the logic of passivity with unparalleled rigor, *The Adventures of David Simple* and *Volume the Last* create an utterly unique character who exposes the disavowed condition of modern agency itself.

No doubt David's passive virtues explicitly recall biblical martyrs. "Like *Job*," David patiently submits to the temporary sufferings allotted him after losing his fortune and moving his family into a humble cottage (261), and while losing his wife, Camilla, David, again like Job, makes himself content with the Almighty. Though he fasts and prays "like his royal Example in the Scripture," King David, while his petition to God could still be granted, when Camilla finally dies, David Simple acquiesces humbly, "satisfied in the Wisdom as well as the Goodness of the great Disposer of Events" (328). And finally the passive, Christ-like virtues of self-sacrifice David originally seeks in a true friend are the same virtues he embodies throughout his own adventures: the virtues of someone whose every action proceeds "either from Obedience to the *Divine Will*" or from the delight he takes in doing good, someone who cannot "see another's Suffering without Pain" (58–59). But Fielding's characterization of humility would be misunderstood if, in the spirit of Hume, we considered it merely an antiquated religious virtue threatening to a modern civil society which, in the wake of a weakened central authority, demanded of men a stronger sense of self in order to secure social and economic order. In fact, David's passive virtues orchestrate the movement of plot through decidedly worldly affairs, including the pivotal juncture where David's ill fortune is sealed by fate.

The fatal moment comes when David allows himself to be persuaded by a faux benefactor, Mr. Ratcliff, to continue defending himself against a bogus and expensive lawsuit launched five years earlier by a man with means who had made a pretended claim to the estate left to David by his uncle. It is worth quoting the key passage at length:

> Now first was *David Simple* seized with some Degree of that Timidity of Mind, which he afterwards more fully experienced; and though in his own Opinion (and in that of the whole Society) it appeared most prudent to keep his Resolution, and drop his Chancery Suite; yet he feared to lose the Favour of a Man, who was so able, and who declared himself so willing to provide amply for his Son: he, therefore,

after much perplexing Deliberation, acquainted Mr. *Ratcliff*, that he would submit to his Judgment, and leave his Cause to the decision of the Law. Mr. *Orguiel* also highly approved Mr. *Ratcliff*'s Advice in this Case, and strenuously urged *David*'s Acquiescence with it; telling him, that a Man of his peculiar way of thinking, ought always, in worldly Affairs, to be directed by Men of Prudence and Experience; hinting, at the same time, how liable he had been, in the former part of his Life, to be imposed on and deceived. (253)

Passive virtues now appear in a decidedly secular situation in which everything turns on the issue of risk management: despite the murmur of his socially sanctioned resolve telling him to pay off his unethical but resourceful legal opponent, David is "seized" with some "timidity of mind," and ultimately "submits" to the judgment of Ratcliff and Orguiel, men who are ostensibly more experienced in worldly affairs. And this language of vulnerability describes David throughout both novels. "Tenderness [is] always predominant in his Mind" (30); he is capable "of the strongest Affection" (103); bad news "deeply imprint[s]" his imagination (272); he is "always ready to expose himself" for the sake of friends (272). At times the vulnerability is explicitly masculine: when he lost his daughter, Fanny, for instance, David "bore it like a Man" (295). At times the vulnerability is obviously feminine, as when David learns of his brother's deceit: while his good-natured uncle plays the man's role and takes care of business, the news overcomes David's already weakened body and he faints away (18). Or when David hears Cynthia's sob story and proves himself extremely sensitive to the suffering of his fellow creatures: "*David's* Tears flowed as fast as hers; his Words could find no Utterance, and he stood motionless as a Statue" (99). In fact, corresponding to the character's vulnerability is his inaction and inability to articulate. After all, David doesn't *do* much in either of the novels; Fielding praises him, if you remember, as a man with no "ambition" (245). And what propels the plot isn't David's activity, but rather his passivity in the face of accidents—accidents that force encounters (44), interrupt tranquility (105), demand patience (254), and pass time (245). Nor does David say much through the course of the novel until the very end, on his deathbed, when his thoughts are presented by Fielding not in a "long-continued Harangue," but passively, in the manner that they "passed in his Mind" and "fell from his Lips" (340). David Simple is a distinctly modern, even postmodern, man without qualities.

But he is not a man living exclusively before or after his time, not simply for us a vision of postmodern personal apathy nor a Christ figure in a contrary commercial world where otherworldly compassion confronts worldly self-interest. That's the point of the passage in which David is persuaded to continue his legal defense in spite of his better judgment. Though it is the passive virtue of humility that turns David's fortune at this critical moment, Fielding takes great care to show how the very commercial, legal, and social system that is used in this case to exploit David's vulnerability depends at its core upon the vulnerability of everyone, including the emotionally hapless Spatter and Orguiel. After all, the case, in all of its cynical calculations of relative financial, legal, and social means, is ultimately about a new culture that increasingly demands of everyone not heroic acts of will, but rather the decidedly unheroic capacity for risk management. As Fielding artfully implies in this critical scene, David Simple isn't an anomaly in the modern world, not a feminized aberration from the norm of a virile public culture, but rather its disavowed precondition. The good news, Fielding might observe, is that this same modern world still holds at its core the passive virtues of humility.

This potentially redemptive irony takes allegorical form in Fielding's *Familiar letters between the characters in David Simple, and some others* (1747),[31] a two-volume collection of forty-five imagined letters, two dialogues, and a final moral allegory, called "A Vision," written by Fielding herself, in which the narrator

---

31. Sarah Fielding, *Familiar letters between the characters in David Simple, and some others. To which is added A vision* (London: Millar, 1747).

has the following dream. The dream, it should be noted, invokes the form of the spiritual quest popularized by John Bunyan's *The Pilgrims Progress*, but now with pointedly secular themes.[32] On a large plain where all of humankind seems assembled stand four gates labeled Wealth, Power, Pleasure, and Virtue, each of which draws eager pilgrims despite the fact that the narrator can read alternative messages beneath the labels on each of the gates: Avarice, Ambition, Disappointment, Pride. In a cumulative experience of illusion and dissolution, the narrator and a host of ultimately selfish fellow travelers visit the palace that lies behind each gate, culminating finally in the palace of Pride, which is swarming with Pride's offspring conceived by incestuous coupling with Pride's five-thousand-year-old father, Folly. The fate of those who find their way to Pride is explained by Deception, whose designated task is literally to affix pictures to reality: "know, that all those Pictures, through which you saw me put the Screws, are hieroglyphical Representations of some Virtue or Faculty of the Mind: for example, that given me by *Insolence*, is a Representation of *Greatness of Mind*...that by *Envy*, of *Penetration*; and so all the rest. I have the Power of screwing into the Bosoms of all who love and caress me, that Picture, of which they make choice. This puts them to great pain, but yet they are so eager to have it done, that they suffer it very patiently."[33] At the heart of those quintessentially modern passions of avarice and ambition that compose the predominant passion of Pride—Hume's constitutive passion without which there could be no modern self—Fielding wisely detects the enabling precondition of humility, personified with unparalleled acuity in her anticharacter David Simple.

What, finally, might be the critical function of such a public, literary display on the part of Fielding? We can begin to answer this question by invoking another asked by Kaja Silverman in

32. Linda Bree, *Sarah Fielding* (New York: Twayne, 1996), 53–55. The following plot summary is essentially Bree's and uses some of Bree's language.

33. Fielding, *Familiar letters*, 385.

Male Subjectivity at the Margins as she too works out a particular politics of psyche.

> What is it precisely that the male masochist displays, and what are the consequences of this self-exposure? To begin with, he acts out in an insistent and exaggerated way the basic conditions of cultural subjectivity, conditions that are normally disavowed; he loudly proclaims that his meaning comes to him from the Other, prostrates himself before the gaze even as he solicits it, exhibits his castration for all to see, and revels in the sacrificial basis of the social contract. The male masochist magnifies the losses and divisions upon which cultural identity is based, refusing to be sutured or recompensed. In short, he radiates a negativity inimical to the social order.[34]

Through the resolutely passive and humiliated character of David Simple, Sarah Fielding reminds all of us moderns that this negativity can, and must, tell its stories.

---

34. Kaja Silverman, *Male Subjectivity at the Margins* (New York: Routledge, 1992), 206.

5

Thinking and Feeling without a Brain: William Perfect and Adam Smith's Compassion

A case study of a man suffering from delusions of grandeur lies at the heart of William Perfect's immensely popular *Annals of Insanity* "Comprising a Selection of Curious and Interesting Cases in the Different Species of Lunacy, Melancholy, or Madness, with the Modes of Practice in the Medical and Moral Treatment, As Adopted in the Cure of Each" (1st ed., 1778; quoted 5th ed., 1809).[1] Case 14, illustrating that "pride is the most dangerous enemy of mankind," captures Perfect the physician, prominent

1. William Perfect, *Annals of Insanity* (New York: Arno Press, 1976). Subsequent citations will be internal according to case number. As Hunter and Macalpine note (citation below), the *Annals* achieved seven editions, which demonstrates a popularity equaled only by the anonymous *A Treatise of Diseases of the Head, Brain & Nerves* (7th ed., 1741) and exceeded only by Robert Burton's *Anatomy of Melancholy*. The *Annals* was the first collection of psychiatric case material, and as such it served as a useful complement to William Battie's *Treatise on madness* (1758) and Thomas Arnold's learned two-volume theoretical text *Classification of mental diseases* (1782). For a brief introduction to Perfect, see the rich resource Richard Hunter and Ida Macalpine, *Three Hundred Years of Psychiatry 1535–1860: A History Presented in Selected English Texts* (London: Oxford University Press, 1963), 501–2.

Freemason, poet, and owner of a private madhouse at West Malling, Kent, in an expansive mood. It thus provides an exceptionally rich starting point for a discussion of the eighteenth-century emergence of psychology as an apolitical discipline.

The patient was a middle-aged man, not tall, but upright in stature, remarkable for acrimony in his speech and answers, impetuousity in his manner, and austerity in his actions. His countenance bore evident traits of pride, suspicion, and moroseness; he was naturally of a restless, contentious, and irritable disposition. From an unexpected miscarriage in his commercial affairs, he became intolerably discontented, jealous, rude, disrespectful to his family, contemptuous, intemperately passionate, and misanthropic to the greatest degree. In this manner his insanity commenced. He drew upon his banker for sums immensely beyond what his accounts would afford, and when disappointed in this respect, became sullen, and immediately issued drafts upon houses with which he never had the least connection, for enormous sums. These and innumerable other actions equally *outrè*, fixed the criterion of his insanity, and determined his relations to take out a statute of lunacy, and to fix him in a place appropriate to his disordered imagination. He issued his mandates and decrees with all the arrogance and self-importance of an eastern despot. He would often draw upon the bank for ten or twenty thousand pounds, with all that settled pomp and gravity which seemed to mark the reality of the transaction. He frequently insisted upon his being the lord chancellor, king of Spain, duke of Batavia, or some other great personage, and accordingly demanded reverence and respect; which homage, if not paid him, he would immediately become surly and outrageous, and with great vociferation would give out his orders for the punishment of those delinquents who appeared to have been remiss in their duty and obedience; and would remain apparently satisfied, as if he thought his commands had been punctually attended to. He seldomly expressed the sense of any bodily pain; nor was bleeding, blistering, vomiting, or any evacuations of the least service: he was uniformly vain, formal, and stately; arrogant, gloomy, and self-sufficient; and however ridiculous his words and actions appear to others, they were supported in himself with all the dignity of excessive pride and ostentation, in the uniform exhibition of that species of insanity with which he was affected. His imaginary greatness and self-consequence dwindled into a total decay, as he approached the verge of idiotism.

Certainly there are moments in this case study that invoke the mechanistic traditions of *medicina mentis* going back to Stoic moral therapy and Galen's humoral pathology.[2] When Perfect makes the Galenic observation that the patient was "naturally of a restless, contentious, and irritable disposition," for instance, we should be prepared to hear that the patient is unmoved by conventional purgatives such as bleeding, blistering, and vomiting, and that he seldom expressed the sense of any bodily pain: these are classic characteristics of people who are irascible by nature. And when Perfect calls the patient "intemperately passionate," we should expect that the case will revolve in Stoic fashion around the successful, or in this case unsuccessful, return to reason. There are also moments in this case study that invoke new sciences emerging alongside Perfect's clinical psychology, such as Johann-Caspar Lavater's immensely influential physiognomic science that purported to provide a key to reading character directly from facial expressions. However, in the analysis that follows, I will focus less upon the mechanical aspects of Perfect's diagnosis and treatment, already discussed extensively in the standard histories of eighteenth-century psychological medicine written by Christopher Fox, Roy Porter, and G. S. Rousseau,[3] and more

2. See especially Galen, *On the Passions and Errors of the Soul*, trans. Paul W. Harkins (Columbus: Ohio State University Press, 1963).

3. Standard secondary sources with a notable historiographic dimension include Christopher D. Green's online database *Classics in the History of Psychology*, available from psychclassics.yorku.ca (accessed April 24, 2005); Roger Smith, *The Norton History of the Human Sciences* (New York: Norton, 1997); Gary Hatfield, "Remaking the Science of Mind: Psychology as Natural Science," in *Inventing Human Science: Eighteenth-Century Domains*, ed. Christopher Fox, Roy Porter, and Robert Wokler (Berkeley: University of California Press, 1995); Fernando Vidal, "Psychology in the 18th Century: A View from Encyclopaedias," *History of the Human Sciences* 6, no. 1 (1993): 89–121; "On Psychology," special issue of *Science in Context* 5, no. 2 (1992); G. S. Rousseau, ed., *The Languages of Psyche: Mind and Body in Enlightenment Thought* (Berkeley: University of California Press, 1990); Roger Smith, "Does the History of Psychology Have a Subject?" *History of the Human Sciences* 1, no. 2 (1988): 147–77; Christopher Fox, ed., *Psychology and Literature*

upon what I will call the eighteenth-century politics of psyche. Most suggestive for the purposes of this study are those social and economic miscues of patient X that, according to Perfect's diagnosis, "fixed the criterion of his insanity."

Rejecting a progressive model that would mine the historical record for evidence of late-modern psychology's absence or presence, the following study instead poses two genealogical questions: What can the eighteenth-century emergence of psychological science tell us about the cultural specificity of "psyche" then and now? And how does this supposedly universal science cover its historical tracks? What is at stake for the social order when a particular version of psyche is defended in universal terms? In order to address these questions, it is helpful to expand the object of my inquiry beyond texts and issues already canonized in the history of psychology to include what might appear at first blush peripheral material—material that can in fact help us read politics back into Perfect's quasi-scientific text. This material might include the case histories of the born again that populated the English and German literary imagination with stories about the relational psyche,[4] the animism of physician Georg Ernst von Stahl and other critics of Cartesian mind/body dualism,[5] and

---

in the Eighteenth Century (New York: AMS Press, 1987). However, none of these sources address what I'm calling in this essay the "politics of psyche."

4. The most prominent examples of these Pietist case histories are collected in Johann Henrich Reitz, *Historie Der Wiedergebohrnen,* ed. Hans-Jürgen Schrader, 4 vols. (Tübingen: Niemeyer, 1982). This collection, originally published serially between 1698 and 1745, relied heavily upon the English Puritan case histories collected by Vavasor Powell, *Spiritual experiences, of sundry beleevers* (London: Ibbitson, 1653). For commentary on the psychological legacy of spiritual autobiography in the German context, see Hans-Jürgen Schings, *Melancholie und Aufklärung: Melancholiker und ihre Kritiker in Erfahrungsseelenkunde und Literatur des 18. Jahrhunderts* (Stuttgart: Metzler, 1977).

5. Stahl's unifying treatment of body and soul directly challenged somatically oriented medicine as well as post-Cartesian philosophy. See Johanna Geyer-Kordesch, "Georg Ernst Stahl's Radical Pietist Medicine and Its Influence on the German Enlightenment," in *The Medical Enlightenment of the Eighteenth Century,* ed. Andrew Cunningham and Roger French (Cambridge: Cambridge University Press, 1990), 67–87. Supporting the Pietist notion that nature could be changed by spiritual rebirth, Stahl argued that matter was "moved" and organized by the soul. Hydraulics of the human

the Puritan and Pietist pedagogy that implicated the relational psyche in the state apparatus.[6] Given the focus of this chapter, however, it will be most helpful to draw upon the moral philosophy of Adam Smith and the Scottish Enlightenment (referred to obliquely in the subtitle of Perfect's book) that, in its metacritical capacity, reflects some of the mechanisms by which psychological individuals were composed. By reading across these neighboring discourses, we can better determine what is at stake, for instance, when Perfect prefaces a case history with the observation that pride is the most dangerous enemy of humankind. We also become more aware of the ways in which the current understanding of the discipline psychology—as well as our popular understanding of the psychological in general—still suffers from an interpretive incapacity.

It should be noted right off that the term *psychology* so used is strictly anachronistic, at least in the English language context. Despite the rarity of the term—it is utterly absent, for instance, in John Locke's *An Essay concerning Human Understanding* nor does it appear anywhere in Hume's substantial corpus—we tend nevertheless to think of the long eighteenth century as a golden age of psychology, when the science of the soul finally shed its spiritual trappings and began to treat the mind as a coherent object of investigation crucial for what it could reveal about the nature of human beings and their particular experience of the world.[7] Present in English only as a specialized term related

---

body might be altered, for instance, by rehabituation, and a physical symptom such as chronic speechlessness cured by an act of retribution directed against the traumatizing agent. See Georg Ernst Stahl, *Über den mannigfaltigen Einfluß von Gemütsbewegungen auf den menschlichen Körper* (Leipzig: Barth, 1961), 26, 31.

6. Mary Fulbrook, *Piety and Politics: Religion and the Rise of Absolutism in England, Württemberg, and Prussia* (Cambridge: Cambridge University Press, 1983).

7. See, for instance, Fox, *Psychology and Literature in the Eighteenth Century*. Roger Smith has taken particular pains to point out that *psychology* is a term circumscribed by the methodological or polemic concerns of the author, which may include telling a speculative story about the history of psyche going back to Aristotle's *De anima* or tracing a *Begriffsgeschichte* to Marko Marulic's *Psichiologia de ratione animae humanae*

to pneumatology, or "knowledge of all spirits, angels, &c.,"[8] *psychology* does not so much as appear in general references such as Samuel Johnson's *A Dictionary of the English Language* (1755 and later editions) or Thomas Sheridan's *A General Dictionary* (1780). Even the novels of Daniel Defoe, Henry Fielding, and Samuel Richardson, typically distinguished from Romance by their new psychological realism,[9] skirt the term.

Does this confusion point to anything significant about our (mis)understanding of eighteenth-century culture and its legacy, or is it merely a semantic problem solved by qualifying our use of the term *psychology* as descriptive if it predates the mid-nineteenth century, natural-scientific version of the discipline? You can guess by the first question that I believe important new horizons for research open when we investigate psyche in eighteenth-century culture without confining ourselves within the bounds of the sciences or the humanities as they are now typically understood. Psychology as a *human* science demands a genealogy that takes seriously its legacy as a practical art designed not simply to describe how the mind works, but rather to formulate psyche as a function of power. We should be reminded, for instance, how the psyche (*anima* in Latin, or *soul* in English) has functioned as a vehicle for ethical and political intervention, whether in the form of neoclassical eloquence, moral philosophy, legal injunction, conduct book, talking cure, or even a novel. In fact, we are guilty of presentism in the most misleading form when we look with blinders to the eighteenth century for hallmarks of latter-day psychology, whether that means a quantitative and descriptive science of the brain or mind, or even a universal notion of the psychological individual. Rendered invisible in this narrow search is the political constitution of psyche—including categories of rank, gender, and

---

(1524?), telling a particular history of an academic discipline or legitimizing a subfield of current psychology, whether experimental, behavioral, social, and so forth.

8. Vidal, "Psychology in the 18th Century."

9. Ian Watt, *The Rise of the Novel: Studies in Defoe, Richardson and Fielding* (Berkeley: University of California Press, 1964).

geography—about which sentimental authors wrote with great care, at the same time that they mused in utopian fashion about a moral sense equally shared by all.

>>><<<

If my hypothesis about the political constitution of psyche is correct, then we should see evidence of it in Perfect's description of the causes of his patient's mental illness. And indeed we do, especially when we read the case study against others in the collection and against Perfect's more speculative observations in the preface. Remember that Perfect begins with the observation that the patient was "naturally of a restless, contentious, and irritable disposition" and that an unexpected miscarriage in his commercial affairs precipitated antisocial behavior: "he became intolerably discontented, jealous, rude, disrespectful to his family, contemptuous, intemperately passionate, and misanthropic to the greatest degree." "In this manner," observes Perfect, "his insanity commenced." The preface to the *Annals* provides a theoretical context for this case by suggesting that the remote causes of insanity consist of two kinds: bodily and mental. Among bodily causes of insanity are irritations of the membranes and vessels of the brain, fevers, worms, constipation, and so forth that might either cause the sort of irritability suffered by patient X or exacerbate his sensitive predisposition. But Perfect devotes more attention and eloquent language to the mental causes of insanity:

> In the latter [i.e., mental causes], various passions, as fanaticism, joy, grief, hatred, anger, jealousy, pride, ill-requited love, misplaced confidence, desertion of friends at a moment, perhaps, when the balm of friendship would have softened poignant sorrow, and the pointed finger of conscious superiority, when the voice of comfort was earnestly and sanguinely expected; these are trials for the human breast infinitely too keen and severe for tender and delicately susceptible minds to combat with; the consequence is, that reason is hurled from her throne, and the greatest skill is often exerted for long time in vain to repair the injury, and wipe away the sense of misfortune.

> *Extreme sensibility* may be deemed a weakness; if so, it is the most amiable, the most pitiable, and most to be deplored of any that ever occasioned mental derangement.

It may seem a stretch to describe irascible patient X as a man of extreme sensibility, but in fact Perfect's general observation about the susceptibility of mind holds even in this case. First and foremost, the patient is susceptible to economic *Fortuna*, the unexpected miscarriage in commercial affairs that apparently precipitates his mental decline; he is susceptible to disappointment at the hands of creditors real and imagined, to the statutes of lunacy, and to his disgruntled relatives who would dispatch him to the madhouse. Once so confined, even the despotic arrogance and self-importance of patient X seems, according to the logic of Perfect's narrative, a delusional overreaction to abject helplessness. This is the brilliance of Perfect's work as an author of popular psychiatric case studies, and it is one of the things we have to relearn in the wake of scientific psychology's later triumph: the psyche is a precipitate of social relations, and as such it is subject to historical variation. But in order to achieve a finer sense of this variation, we must remember to distinguish Perfect's social passions from more familiar Cartesian emotions. According to Perfect, the trials for the human breast that can overwhelm susceptible minds are the various passions such as fanaticism, joy, grief, hatred, anger, jealousy, pride, ill-requited love, misplaced confidence, as well as the compassion that fails when one is deserted by friends or accused "with the pointed finger of conscious superiority"—social passions, in other words, not the individual instantiations of universally shared emotions that captured Descartes's imagination, as I discussed in chapter 1, and that are still considered "primary" by leading neurophysiologists such as Antonio Damasio. A sample of Perfect's case histories bears out this distinction.

Mrs. E. H. (case 23) is described by Perfect as a woman remarkable for the size of her head who had "been made a proselyte to a prevailing system of religion [Methodism], that like an epidemic

disease had long spread its baneful influence through many ranks
of people, to the excitement of the most daring outrages, and the
wildest extravagancies." This religious enthusiasm, or fanaticism,
which Perfect treats both as a traumatic cause of mental illness
and a cultural formation that fixes the criterion of the patient's
insanity (to recall a familiar formula), provokes from Perfect ex-
tensive commentary that can be organized under three general
headings applicable across the range of case studies. (1) *Psyche is
composed as the imagined object of another's love or hatred.* In this
case, the patient imagines herself the object not of a loving but of
a terrible God, who is represented as "inthroned in heaven, de-
lighting in the punishment of his weak and helpless creatures."
(2) *Psyche is composed in language and is thus susceptible to another's
rhetoric.* Deserting in this case the plain and simple paths of the
gospel, Mrs. E. H.'s fancy was fed with "unintelligible jargon"
that perplexed her brain. And finally (3) the *excessive sensibility*
personified with particular intensity in modern women and the
idle rich makes these souls particularly vulnerable limit cases for
the general population. In fact, Perfect implicates this case in
a larger historical and sociological context, remarking that instances of insanity are more numerous at this time and in this
kingdom than any former period. The principal cause for this
increase, ventures Perfect in the spirit of English cultural critics going back at least to Joseph Addison and Richard Steele, is
the epidemic religious enthusiasm that degrades the reasoning
faculties and the "present universal diffusion of wealth of luxury through almost every part of the kingdom." This observation
is then corroborated in the series of cases in which would-be
scholars and pillars of society devolve into melancholia as they
retire or otherwise separate themselves from normal social activity
(cases 10 and 18) or the whims of well-to-do women are indulged
to the point that they lose all sense of reality (case 20). Suffering from the social passion of fanaticism, then, one might expect
that Mrs. E. H. would be subject to a social—or in contemporary
language a "moral"—cure. And this is in fact what Perfect pre-
scribes, with notable success. Though her wild antics and religious

reveries were mitigated by an abstemious diet, bleeding, laxatives, and other measures designed to direct her blood to "cooler channels," Perfect attributes the abatement of her symptoms primarily to a radical shift in social context. Once the access to her person enjoyed by "sanctified sectaries" was restored to her family and the flow of Methodist principles shut off at the source, Mrs. E. H.'s enthusiastic raptures "began gradually to lose their influence on her mind."

And like fanaticism, the other passions that populate Perfect's case histories are inherently social, or relational. Thus, for instance, grief might be characterized as the traumatic loss of a near relation (cases 7 and 12), ill-requited love as matrimonial disappointment (case 2), and misplaced confidence as a woman mistaken in the "apprehension of the fidelity of her husband" (case 4). Compassion, however, is a social passion that separates itself from the others because it implicates directly not only the patient in his or her social setting, but also the "spectator" as a privileged agent in an economy of emotional scarcity. Just as Adam Smith had urged the "indifferent spectator" in his *The Theory of Moral Sentiments* a few decades earlier,[10] a sentimental William Perfect challenges both medical doctors and his lay readers to "feel another's woe" and treat the object of suffering with compassion. Since mental illness can be characterized as the mismatch of emotion to circumstance, we can always help ourselves and help each other by simply remaining in contact with one another. Expressing a theory that would become instrumental for Perfect's moral cure, Smith ventures that "society and conversation, therefore, are the most powerful remedies for restoring the mind to its tranquility" (24). But when we analyze more closely the language and narrative arc of Perfect's case studies—or any sentimental literature for that matter—we see that compassion still functions unevenly.

10. Adam Smith, *The Theory of Moral Sentiments* (Amherst: Prometheus Books, 2000), 5.

As I indicated at the outset of this chapter, case 14, which introduces the prideful patient X, provokes from Perfect a stream of related stories and general commentary, most of which revolves around the issue of compassion. Interestingly, Perfect premises the relation between analogous cases by observing that, although insanity might be the most terrible infirmity to which human nature is subject, the calamity in fact appears more terrible to the spectator than it really is, because the spectator mistakenly "judges of the feelings of the unfortunate by his own, conceiving what himself, endowed with reason, would experience, if in his situation." And though this disconnect between spectator and patient, reason and insanity, sometimes provokes bemusement, Perfect reassures the spectator not to feel ashamed, for "the tear of pity will not flow less sincerely down the cheek of sensibility, because alternately blended with involuntary laughter." As proof of this assertion, Perfect adds another story about a poor man who had studied the art of government and the balance of European power while neglecting his business, became insane, and fancied himself king. Admitted into the workhouse of St. Giles in the Fields, the imaginary monarch appointed an "idiot" to be simultaneously prime minister, barber, and menial servants; thereafter, the two could be seen issuing precepts to their imaginary subjects. Expelled by the sovereign one day for eating breakfast first, the "degraded minister" caught a fever and died. This had such an effect upon the fancied king that, after having lived almost without sustenance and in a continued silence, "he actually died of grief."

Now compare Perfect's self-consciously compassionate presentation of these related cases of excessive pride to case 26, the story of an "unhappy object" confined to a workhouse by the parish officers of Friendbury:

> In the year 1776, the parish officers of Friendbury applied to me for advice in the case of a maniacal patient confined in their workhouse. This unhappy object had been very desperate, and had committed many acts of outrage and violence; was naturally of a strong, muscular

shape, and rendered much stronger by his present complaint. He had overpowered almost every one before they could properly secure him, which was now effected in a very extraordinary manner. He was fastened to the floor by means of an iron ring, which was tied to a pair of fetters about his legs, and he was hand-cuffed. The place of his confinement was a large lower room, occasionally made use of for a kitchen, and which opened into the street; their wooden bars to the windows, through the spaces of which continual visitors were observing, pointing at, ridiculing, and irritating the poor maniac, who thus became a spectacle of public sport and amusement. . . . I was requested to take him immediately home to my house; but as the poor wretch was in a highly infuriated state, and that in great measure occasioned by the unsuitableness of his situation, my advice was to take off his shackles, and secure him in a strong strait-waistcoat. . . . Besides this, I directed the surgeon, who had the superintendance of the poor, to keep his head closely shaved, to bleed him ad deliquium. . . . These instructions were effectually put into practice; and proper attention being thus paid to his person and diet, in a few weeks the patient intirely recovered his reason; and begging hard to be released from his confinement, after I had been again consulted, it was granted, when he quietly and regularly returned to his labour and employment; and I have not heard of his having had any relapse.

Where privileged patient X, if you remember, was remarkable for "acrimony in his speech and answers, impetuousity in his manner, and austerity in his actions"—that is to say, for his psychological ill-disposition toward the world around him—brutish patient Y was remarkable for his violent behavior. Where the excessively prideful soul of patient X would be read by way of his countenance, the dangerous body of patient Y would be read by way of his muscular shape. Where the deficiencies of patient X as an economic agent fixed the conditions of his insanity, iron rings, fetters, and taunting spectators fixed the conditions of patient Y's insanity. And finally, where a "valuable member of society" is restored to his rational faculty (case 10) and a woman to her family (case 4), patient Y is returned to his labor.

My point is not simply that Perfect as a doctor of his time treats patients differently according to their class status, nor that a patient's ability to pay affects his or her treatment, nor simply that a kind of Foucauldian discipline is most obvious when it applies to the socially disadvantaged. All of these observations may be true, but for my purposes they are unremarkable. Rather, my point is that, as a doctor of his time, Perfect *lacks the very notion* of a universal, psychological individual of the sort we project back into the Enlightenment. Admittedly, Perfect echoes many of his contemporaries by referring to rational man, and even his unhappy object Y is finally restored to reason when proper attention is paid to his person and diet. I am suggesting, however, that in this case Perfect exploits the return to reason more as an alibi for functional success than as an end in itself, as he claims in the preface. And in so doing, Perfect is in harmony with his Enlightenment contemporaries, from Thomas Hobbes and John Locke to Adam Smith and Mary Wollstonecraft, who are misleadingly considered prophets of a universal, psychological individual.

A Theory of Moral Sentiments

To read the opening passage of Adam Smith's *The Theory of Moral Sentiments* (1759) is to encounter firsthand this specter of universal psychology bequeathed, supposedly, by the Scottish Enlightenment and at the same time establish the primary reference point for William Perfect's moral philosophy. It is a passage on sympathy typically, and understandably, read against the grain of Smith's remarkably pessimistic analysis that follows, and as such it provides an opportunity to see precisely where our more sentimental readings of such literature start to go wrong.

In an opening passage that would challenge a Hobbes or a Bernard de Mandeville, Smith begins:

> How selfish soever man may be supposed, there are evidently some principles in his nature, which interest him in the fortune of others, and render their happiness necessary to him, though he derives

nothing from it, except the pleasure of seeing it. Of this kind is pity or compassion, the emotion which we feel for the misery of others, when we either see it, or are made to conceive it in a very lively manner. That we often derive sorrow from the sorrow of others, is a matter of fact too obvious to require any instances to prove it; for this sentiment, like all the other original passions of human nature, is by no means confined to the virtuous and humane, though they perhaps may feel it with the most exquisite sensibility. The greatest ruffian, the most hardened violator of the law of society, is not altogether without it. (3)

In no uncertain terms, Smith invokes original passions of human nature—such as the moral sentiment of compassion—that may be felt more exquisitely by some, but are ultimately shared by all. And later, in a chapter on "universal benevolence," we do see Smith attribute these original passions of human nature to the good graces of a benevolent Being determined to maintain the greatest possible quantity of happiness (345). No doubt the contrary idea of a "mischievous being" naturally provokes our hatred, but even in this case the ill-will we bear toward the hated object is still the consequence of our universal benevolence because, as Smith explains, it is motivated by the sympathy we feel for those innocents (like ourselves) whose happiness is disturbed. The purpose of civilization, then, is to indulge our benevolent affections that constitute the perfection of human nature (27) and, by acting according to the dictates of our moral faculties that serve as intuitive guides, promote nature's objective with ever-increasing precision (239). So when one of our brain scientists of emotion, Antonio Damasio, muses that the history of civilization is, to some extent, "the history of a persuasive effort to extend the best of 'moral sentiments' to wider and wider circles of humanity," we are not surprised to find Adam Smith cited as an intellectual antecedent.[11] Like Smith, it would seem, Damasio would be hard-pressed to recognize political economies of emotion of the sort I've been describing throughout this book,

---

11. Damasio, *Looking for Spinoza*, 163 (see chap. 1, n. 13).

where emotion is essentially a function of social difference. For even the greatest ruffian and the most hardened violator of the laws of society is not altogether without compassion, according to Smith, and presumably that kernel of compassion planted in everyone by God (or, alternatively, biology) can be cultivated to the point where universal benevolence prevails. Social difference and social antagonism do indeed exist, but they seem to be mere pathologies of an increasingly benevolent world driven by what Smith would later call famously "The Invisible Hand"[12] and what Damasio would consider a consequence of evolutionary biology.

If only it were so easy. What, after all, is the purpose of Smith's 538-page treatise if moral sentiments are already distributed to everyone and invested with the natural impulse toward a greater good? This would make for a boring book indeed. Shouldn't benevolence eventually find its own way without the help of intricate theories and arduous programs of reform? Like other engaging works of Enlightenment and sensibility we have thus far examined, including David Hume's *A Treatise of Human Nature*, Sarah Fielding's *The Adventures of David Simple*, and William Perfect's *Annals of Insanity*, Smith's *The Theory of Moral Sentiments* ultimately depends upon the inherent drama of emotions unevenly distributed across rank and gender in particular. Smith's emotions are also specific in their geographic and historical constitution (different, for example, across the civilized and the savage) and, as the product of changeable human institutions (such as laws, prisons, and palaces), are social phenomena contestable over time. Chapter headings are telling: "Of the Origin of Ambition, and the Distinction of Ranks," "Of the Corruption of Our Moral Sentiments, Which Is Occasioned by This Disposition to Admire the Rich and the Great, and to Despise or Neglect Persons of Poor and Mean Condition," "Of the Influence of Custom and Fashion upon Moral Sentiments," "Of the Order in Which Individuals Are Recommended by Nature

12. See also Smith, *Theory of Moral Sentiments*, 126, 235, and 238.

to Our Care and Attention." For Smith, universal beneficence is clearly not the end of the story, nor is some notion of natural equality, nor is nature per se. Even the moral sentiments that seem securely implanted by God turn out to be corruptible by our mundane disposition to admire the rich and the great and to despise or neglect the poor. Put another way, Smith's project of improving our moral condition depends upon the rhetorical commonplace first articulated by Aristotle that emotion is a matter of propriety, and propriety is, in turn, a matter of social difference. According to Aristotle, when we speak of anger, for instance, we need to know "what is their *state of mind* when people are angry and against *whom* are they usually angry, and for what sort of *reasons*" (*Rhetoric*, 2.1.8). Or in Smith's charming formulation, a severe tragedy such as a sudden fall into poverty may deserve sympathy, whereas failure of one's cook or butler in the least article of their duty doesn't (57); a sudden fall into disease may deserve sympathy, whereas being jilted by one's mistress or henpecked by one's wife doesn't (59). In each case, the emotion constituted between subject and object is calibrated by the indifferent spectator's sense of propriety, which, as we can surmise from these few examples, is more the commonsense view from a position of social privilege than it is some abstract view from nowhere. Far from a symmetrical phenomenon felt equally by everyone for everyone else, for Smith (as for other sentimental authors such as Sarah Fielding or Laurence Sterne) sympathy is precisely about negotiating social difference *from a particular perspective* (sympathy from whom? for whom? clearly not from the perspective of the cook or the butler or the mistress or the wife, who merely trigger the sympathetic situation) and *in a particular circumstance* where some commonsense notion of propriety prevails. Interesting, then, is the way in which changing contours of emotional propriety and impropriety cut across character and circumstance, as this dynamic might be portrayed in works of literary fiction, or for that matter in a treatise such as *The Theory of Moral Sentiments*, which is an interesting book indeed.

In Smith's scheme, interesting truly matters. For emotions do not simply represent themselves unequivocally through the face or the voice or the gesture, as Descartes or more recent psychologists in the tradition of Paul Ekman would insist. Emotions, for Smith, are essentially communicative, and communication is a vexed, interpretive undertaking designed to draw people's attention to some things and not to others—what Smith calls in the rhetorical tradition the principle of liveliness, or "vivacity" (4). Successful communication, according to both Aristotle and Smith, demands vivid representation, which is an art practiced by everybody who communicates, but mastered especially by the rhetorician and the authors of fictional narrative. In order to be moved by the grief or joy of another—and there is ultimately no purpose for emotion other than to move people—we must be informed of the cause and be familiar with the relevant characters. For instance, Smith makes the distinctly Aristotelian observation that the furious behavior of an angry man is more likely to exasperate us than produce sympathy unless we are adequately acquainted with his provocation, plainly seeing "what is the situation of those with whom he is angry, and to what violence they may be exposed from so enraged an adversary" (6). These are practically Aristotle's words from the *Rhetoric*, verbatim.

"Sympathy," Smith summarizes, "does not arise so much from the view of the passion, as from that of the situation which excites it" (7), and therefore (we may conclude) a moral society where sympathy predominates will also be a literate society where the dramatist and the rhetorician play an important role. Here is Smith's telling example, which among other things shows how the uneven distribution of emotion across gender is not a natural, but rather a literary phenomenon.

> The reserve which the laws of society impose upon the fair sex, with regard to this weakness [i.e., passionate love], renders it more particularly distressful in them, and, upon that very account, more deeply interesting. We are charmed with the love of Phaedra, as it is expressed in the French tragedy of that name, notwithstanding all

the extravagance and guilt which attend it. That very extravagance and guilt may be said, in some measure, to recommend it to us. Her fear, her shame, her remorse, her horror, her despair, become thereby more natural and interesting. (41)

"Interesting" in this case applies not to a set of proper emotions already tailored to circumstance, but to extravagant emotions such as Phaedra's fear, shame, remorse, horror, and despair rendered natural (and thereby appropriate) by the art of the dramatist. A woman's natural weakness for extravagant love is not interesting, but the distress provoked by witnessing the violation of a woman's socially mandated reserve is. Moreover, this literary analysis of emotion is not just a curious supplement to Smith's more serious project, where natural emotions would prevail. Emotion is social all the way down. In a critical chapter on the origin of ambition and the distinction of ranks, Smith considers why the poor man is ashamed of his poverty, while the rich man provokes our admiration. It is not because poverty is condemned by God or nature, whereas wealth is endorsed. It is because, in the end, the poor man goes out and comes in unheeded (71), whereas the man of fortune and rank captures our imagination; his likes and dislikes matter, his actions are the objects of public care. "Scarce a word, scarce a gesture, can fall from him that is altogether neglected," continues Smith, "in a great assembly he is the person upon whom all direct their eyes; it is upon him that their passions seem all to wait with expectation" (72).

Passion, in other words, is a function of publicity. Though fictional drama puts into relief how economies of emotion work, the same principles of publicity (and complementary silence) operate in everyday life. "It is the misfortune of kings only which afford the proper subjects for tragedy," observes Smith in the tradition of Aristotle's *Poetics* and Augustan literary criticism, because "every calamity that befalls them, every injury that is done them, excites in the breast of the spectator ten times more compassion and resentment than he would have felt, had the same thing happened to other men." But similarly, remarks Smith, in the drama of everyday life "all the innocent blood that was shed in the civil wars, provoked less indignation than the death of Charles I" (73).[13]

This disproportion across the social field must be accounted for, moreover, by any would-be therapist. Just as a good therapist like William Perfect must consider the emotional circumstances of a mentally ill patient (one wouldn't, for instance, treat the religious fanatic by securing her in a strong strait-waistcoat and shaving her head, or advise that the violent workingman read La Bruyère), a good therapist of the body politic must consider the emotional circumstances of his subjects. Particularly dangerous, Smith observes, is the politician who is a "man of system" so enamored with the supposed beauty of his own ideal plan of government that he cannot suffer the slightest deviation. Such a politician "goes on to establish it completely and in all its parts, without any regard either to the great interests or to the strong prejudices which may oppose it," behaving as if his subjects are chess pieces with no motion of their own (342–43).[14] For Adam Smith, moreover, there are severe consequences when insensitive legislators try to plow under the emotional contours of a social field. Although the game of human society goes on "easily and harmoniously" if motions of the people and the politicians coincide, if they are opposite or different, "the game will go on miserably, and the society must be at all times in the highest

13. Again in our age, one might consider the disproportionate grief provoked by the death of Princess Di.

14. Looking ahead to our day, one might consider a challenge of multiculturalism such as affirmative action. The man of system opposed to affirmative action might argue that prioritizing objective criteria such as college boards best promotes equal opportunity in college admissions. The Smithian therapist of the body politic, in contrast, would support affirmative action policies, arguing that equal opportunity can best be achieved by accounting directly for different and often conflicting affective histories that cut across a range of subcultures and ethnicities. Affirmative action policies would redistribute emotion more fairly in an economy of scarcity. The excessive pride of white privilege would be contained by exposing as *interested* supposedly neutral cultural institutions such as the SAT or the English literary canon, while black pride would be built by way of an Afrocentrism that privileged the history of the black Diaspora, or ebonics over "standard English."

degree of disorder" (343). When Smith himself is read as a man of system rather than a political economist of emotion, I would add, this lesson is lost.

It turns out that Adam Smith is more like the Thomas Hobbes presented in chapter 1 than he might admit. Since by definition there is never enough glory to go around, what Hobbes and Smith both call *vain*glory is built into the very fabric of society (210, 372). Rather than anchoring social passions in a moral sense equally shared by all, Smith follows Aristotle and Seneca and Hobbes and Hume in sketching an economy of emotional scarcity, a zero-sum game where the emotional wealth of one social agent necessarily comes at the expense of another. Compounding this human tragedy for Hobbes, if you remember, is that people are by nature provided the "multiplying glasses" that distort social relations, whereas they naturally lack the "prospective glasses" that would correct them: namely, moral and civil science. Hobbes sees it precisely as his task in the *Leviathan* to provide the unnatural science that would correct social passions toward adequate civil obedience. Likewise for Smith, passions are unfairly distributed, but at least moral and civil science can help us manage how inequity can be mobilized for the sake of peace.

And in Smith's case, passions must be mobilized for the sake of prosperity as well. Indeed, the new focus on general prosperity and the bourgeois virtues it requires ultimately mark the essential difference between Hobbes's political economy of emotion, circa 1640, and Smith's, over a century later. Unlike either the man of distinction whose glory consists in "the propriety of his ordinary behavior" such as figuring nicely at a ball (78) or the "rude vulgar of mankind" whose physical vulnerability requires that they feel almost nothing (28), the man of middling rank can afford to cultivate those bourgeois sensibilities—compassion first among them—that constitute a civilized nation. "Before we can feel much for others," Smith admits in a passage that dramatically qualifies his universalism, "we must in some measure be at ease ourselves" (297), and ease for Smith includes social stability as well as reliable relief from material concerns such as food, clothing, and shelter. Whereas the man of high rank tends to provoke admiration disproportionately and the man of low rank pity, or ridicule, or nothing at all, the private man of middling rank cultivates those mediocre emotions such as romantic love (290), magnanimity (50), and a decidedly masculine form of compassion called "generosity" that requires not just exquisite fellow-feeling, but self-sacrifice (274): all of which are emotions that strengthen the social bond and ultimately make social investments more secure. And just as William Perfect treated the constitution of psyche differently in the man of business and the man of labor, Adam Smith carefully differentiates psyche according to both rank and profession. "As different objects ought, upon common occasions, to occupy the attention of men of different professions," Smith observes, "so different passions ought naturally to become habitual to them." For example, Smith ventures,

> we cannot expect the same sensibility to the gay pleasures and amusements of life in a clergyman which we lay our account with in an officer. The man whose peculiar occupation is to keep the world in mind of that awful futurity which awaits them, who is to announce what may be the fatal consequences of every deviation from the rules of duty, and who is himself to set the example of the most exact conformity, seems to be the messenger of tidings which cannot, in propriety, be delivered either with levity or indifference. (293–94)[15]

Note, finally, that "exact conformity" means in this case that character must be more than the competent performance of the passions proper to our station, a performance that overlays ostensibly deeper passions more appropriate to our nature. We are, in Sarah Fielding's words, an "exact pattern" of the dominant

15. For a similar observation in our world, see the classic study by sociologist Arlie Russell Hochschild, *The Managed Heart: Commercialization of Human Feeling* (Berkeley: University of California Press, 2003). Although she romanticizes a private sphere of authentic feelings and unalienated selves, Hochschild nonetheless investigates with great sensitivity the ways in which late capitalism requires of service workers particular emotional styles: for instance, in the smile of the flight attendant.

emotions that characterize our place in the world, and any deviation from this pattern represents not a return to some previous human nature enjoyed by all, but rather a negotiation of that social station we are expected to perform.

>>><<<

It is distracting to assume that, for thinkers of the Enlightenment, "rational man" somehow was presumed to reside, even potentially, equally and to the same degree in every human being, whether man or woman, European or savage, adult or child, noble or simpleton. In fact, we can understand the Enlightenment with much more precision when we assume that reason and passion function in an economy of scarcity rather than a natural distribution and then ask how this economy functions in any particular case. When, finally, I apply my revisionist reading of Adam Smith to compare the treatment of Perfect's patient X (the failed businessman) to patient Y (the violent workman), it is clear that the issue turns not on the equitable distribution of psychological care—which might be our own humanitarian concern—but rather on the inequitable distribution of passions and the forms of psyche that results. Simply put, patient X suffers from a range of passions contributing to the condition of excessive pride, whereas patient Y has a negligible emotional life; patient X has a convoluted psyche, whereas for all intents and purposes patient Y has no psyche at all—instead, he has a threatening body. Finally, the spectator is urged to feel compassion toward patient X, an object of suffering more or less equal to the implied spectator/reader, whereas the socially superior spectator of patient Y is urged to feel pity toward an unhappy object.

Emotions, whether in the context of eighteenth-century psychology or even in our own popular psychology, must be read as markers of social distinction rather than just as expressions of a human nature essentially shared by all. Instead of wondering perennially why it has taken so long to extend the range of human compassion to women, to slaves, to non-Europeans, to the poor, to the disabled, and so on, we would do better to track the history of terms such as *pride*, *humility*, *pity*, and *compassion* and see how they have been mobilized for strategic purposes; how, for instance, particular communities are composed by the notion that they have a monopoly on that compassion that would be extended to others. This would be a very different history of psychology indeed.

Index

absolute power, 56n11

absolutism, 58

abstinence, 82, 83

Abu-Lughod, Lila, 6n7

actions: causes of, 40–41; potential and, 98; revolution and, 96n20, 103n30; virtue of, 142. *See also* motion; *movere*

active life (*vita activa*), 86

activism: masculine, 110; post-1960s, 110; reform and, 85–87, 94; Walzer's view of, 87

activity: causation, 24; movement and, 60; passivity and, 87–88, 100; scientific knowledge and, 96–97

actuated man, 136, 140, 141, 145

Addison, Joseph, 165

admiration, 41, 177

Adolphs, Ralph, 31n10

Adventures of David Simple, The (Sarah Fielding). See *David Simple, The Adventures of* (Sarah Fielding)

affect, 9n9, 53n4, 55, 145. *See also* passions

affections: corruption of, 101; psychology of, 123

affirmative action, 175n14

Age of Reason, 55

Age of Sensibility, 8, 131, 149. *See also* sensibility

altruistic behaviors, 75

ambition, 77, 144–56

amygdala, 26, 27, 29–32, 72

anger: apathy and, 67–68; Aristotle on, 1–5; asymmetrical power and, 3; avoidance of, 66–67; beneficial, 43; combating, 25; defensive use of, 38; defined in Aristotle's *Rhetoric*, 1; limitations on, 5; melancholia and, 135; physical manifestations of, 2; pride and, 16; public forms of, 79; response to, 173; social aspects of, 2; social status and, 69; threats and, 16

anger management, 67, 73

anima. See *De anima* (Aristotle); psyche; soul

animal spirits, 27